the SEASONED Life

the SEAS🍲NED Life

FOOD, FAMILY, FAITH, AND THE JOY OF EATING WELL

Ayesha Alexander Curry

LITTLE, BROWN AND COMPANY
New York • Boston • London

Little, Brown and Company
Hachette Book Group
1290 Avenue of the Americas, New York, NY 10104
littlebrown.com

First Edition: September 2016

Little, Brown and Company is a division of Hachette Book Group, Inc. The Little, Brown name and logo are trademarks of Hachette Book Group, Inc.

The publisher is not responsible for websites (or their content) that are not owned by the publisher.

The Hachette Speakers Bureau provides a wide range of authors for speaking events. To find out more, go to hachettespeakersbureau.com or call (866) 376-6591.

Photography by Caroline Egan

Library of Congress Cataloging-in-Publication Data
Names: Curry, Ayesha, author.
Title: The seasoned life: food, family, faith, and the joy of eating well / Ayesha Curry.
Description: First edition. | New York: Little, Brown and Company, [2016] | Includes index.
Identifiers: LCCN 2016010146 | ISBN 978-0-316-31633-0 (hc) / 978-0-316-46705-6 (signed ed)
Subjects: LCSH: Cooking. | Gastronomy. | LCGFT: Cookbooks.
Classification: LCC TX714 .C86 2016 | DDC 641.5—dc23 LC record available at https://lccn.loc.gov/2016010146

10 9 8 7 6 5 4 3 2 1

WOR

Printed in the United States of America

Dedicated to my two beautiful daughters, Riley and Ryan:
that you one day find and fall in love with food and the way it
brings people together, just as I did as a little girl.
Never give up and never take no for an answer when it comes to
following your dreams, goals, and passions.

Contents

the

SEAS⦰NED

Life

Introduction

{ LIVING THE
SEASONED LIFE

G OOD FOOD has the power to make the moment. I grew up in a Toronto suburb called Markham, and my mom had a salon set up in the basement of our home. When I was 6 or 7 years old, I remember sitting in the kitchen of our home, watching my sitter, Dora, make Trinidadian curry and *roti* for my mom's clients every Saturday. I would run back and forth from the basement to the kitchen passing out the warm, wrapped-up *roti*. Good food made everyone okay with the occasional wait.

Growing up in Toronto, I took it for granted that it was perfectly normal for people from every corner of the world to live together. In our neighborhood, there were northern Indian restaurants on nearly every corner. And if it wasn't Indian, it was a restaurant serving Ethiopian, Greek, or the best darn Chinese food you've ever tasted.

This melting pot culture made me feel right at home with my Jamaican-Chinese-Polish-African American heritage. (At school, kids called me "The United Nations.") But when I was 14 years old, our family moved to Charlotte, North Carolina. It was a big change, but a good one. I'm now a lover of biscuits and sweet tea! North Carolina is also where I first encountered the best barbecue I've ever tasted. Today, I like to say that I am a passionate dual citizen: I love both my home countries—and their food.

It was back in Toronto, surrounded by amazing flavors from all over the world, when I first really started getting into food. By my 13th birthday, all I wanted to do was cook! So instead of a dance party, I threw a cooking party. I'm certain my friends showed up expecting to dance and play games. Instead, I put them to work in the kitchen. My wonderful (and patient) parents provided all the ingredients so I could cook the day away with my friends—many of whom I'm still close to today. One memory stands out above the others from that day. I had one friend who decided she was going to rinse off the ground beef to ensure it was clean. Whoops—let's just say that washing ground meat is not a good way to go! But it was hilarious. To this day I think about that incident every time I cook ground beef.

No matter where we lived, the highlight of my food memories was always my mom's cooking. My mom and grandma were born in Jamaica, and although they moved to Canada when my mom was a little girl, they kept island flavors alive at home. My mom would meticulously prepare every meal—brown sugar chicken, soup, rice and peas—even though this meant cooking in big batches for our army-sized gang, including my siblings as well as the many family and friends who would often stop by.

If it wasn't my mom's cooking, we'd be treated to something made by my dad, who grew up in Buffalo, New York. I still think that my dad's signature dish—meat loaf drizzled with a simple but decadent ketchup glaze and topped with a cross made out of green onions—is the best meat loaf ever. The kitchen table was the place where we had our best (and worst) conversations. It's where we spoke about our dreams, reflected on life lessons, and were, let's say, enlightened on how to correct our failures. I have two younger brothers and two older sisters, so you can imagine that chaos was a part of the package deal at dinner. Still, it was a beautiful thing that we could always "press pause" in our hectic lives and come together at the table. It's the reason I feel it's so important to cook for my family today, gathering everyone around the table for a meal. I want to give my husband, Stephen, and our two baby girls, Riley and Ryan, time to disconnect from the world and connect with each other.

When I was 17, I moved to Los Angeles to pursue acting. For me, it was like going to college, and I had to learn how to fend for myself. In LA, I missed my mom's home cooking, especially considering that my meals now included a heavy rotation of instant ramen noodles. It made me want to cook for myself even more. I had success landing acting jobs in LA, but ultimately it didn't feel like the place I was supposed to be. So, after a year and a half, I moved back home. Even so, I am grateful for having had that experience.

It was shortly before moving back to North Carolina that I went on my first real date with Stephen, who was in LA for an event. We'd known each other since we were 14 and 15 years old through our church in North Carolina, but we didn't start dating until many years later. Our interactions up until that point had consisted of phone conversations about Canadian candy (fuzzy peaches are both of our favorites), and the occasional nervous glance at Wednesday night church youth group. And then, out of the blue, he asked me (through Facebook—don't laugh) if I wanted to hang out. We spent the day drinking chai lattes and checking out the stars on Hollywood Boulevard. It was one of the best days ever. A month later, back in Charlotte, he invited me over to his parents' house for chai lattes. I walked into the kitchen and saw a pot on the stove simmering away. It looked like he had made it all himself, and I was impressed. And then his sister came into the room and asked him why he had an empty container of dog

food on the counter. It turned out that the container was hiding the source of the lattes—two Starbucks cups! For a while there, he really had me going.

The rest is truly history. We were inseparable from that day forward. (Although it definitely wasn't because of the "homemade" chai lattes, that's for sure.) On July 30, 2011, we tied the knot at the same church where we had met and spent all those Wednesday nights together as teenagers.

Moving to the San Francisco Bay Area started us on an entirely new adventure. In the Bay Area, I started to get even more determined to learn about food. I even challenged myself to conquer one of my fears—poaching eggs—by taking cooking classes at the San Francisco Cooking School. (Although you won't find any recipes that require poaching eggs in this book; it still makes me a little nervous.)

On July 19, 2012, I gave birth to our first daughter, Riley, and my life changed forever. The shift to motherhood was much easier than I had anticipated, and has been the ultimate blessing. In a way, I get to live life vicariously through her—her first experiences, her first tastes—and each day brings a new adventure. Watching Riley play in her toy kitchen, sneaking into the pantry to collect real food (which will ultimately destroy the toy KitchenAid mixer), is the best kind of entertainment. We welcomed our second little mama, Ryan, in 2015, expanding our new little Curry clan to four.

Anyone who knows our family knows we are extremely down to earth and relaxed. When you walk into our home, the first thing you'll see are toys scattered everywhere. Our Labradoodle, Reza, will barrel toward you to welcome you in. It's perfectly disorganized—and we wouldn't have it any other way. My husband and I are, after all, two young parents in our twenties just trying to figure it all out and, above all, make sure we raise our little family in a happy, healthy home full of faith and love.

While working on this book, I came across a beautiful Maya Angelou quote that perfectly explains the reason why I cook for my family and friends—and why I wanted to do this book. She said:

"I've learned that whenever I decide something with an open heart, I usually make the right decision. I've learned that even when I have pains, I don't have to be one. I've learned that every day you should reach out and touch someone. People love a warm hug or just a friendly pat on the back. I've learned that people will forget what you said, people will forget what you did, but people will never forget how you made them feel."

Everything warm, everything delightful, and everything that is loved in my life somehow involves (and revolves around) food. Still, I can't tell you how many nights I sat up pondering what was going to be the next step in my career. And the answer was staring me in the face all along. This book is the result of a decision I made with an open heart. The support of my family and my faith in God helped me take a giant leap into the unknown as I learned how to turn my love of cooking into a career. I light up every time I get the blend of flavors in a recipe just right, or when I achieve a perfect sear on a steak, or smell a batch of cookies baking. I always enjoy watching the faces of family and friends as they take that first bite.

I wrote this book to share all the wonderful recipes that have made my family happy and satisfied over the years. It's a collection of family favorites from Canada and North Carolina as well as recipes inspired by some of my favorite restaurant dishes. But some are new favorites, too—like the pasta dishes we eat before a game or the California-style salads I've started creating in the past couple of years. They're all fresh and approachable but, most importantly, they encompass all the precious moments that season my life.

The Best Breakfasts

MORNINGS IN MY HOUSE are hit or miss depending on how the night before went. Bedtime with little ones is no joke. We make it as fun and lighthearted as possible and always try to find the silver linings to difficult bedtime routines (and everything else). Needless to say, lavish breakfasts are not always (or even usually!) the norm at our house.

That's perfectly fine with me. I like a quick and simple breakfast, the kind that jumpstarts the day for the whole family. It's how I grew up. My mom always made her Jamaican-spiced cornmeal porridge for me and my siblings, and while I didn't necessarily appreciate it at the time, it certainly fueled our days. These types of breakfasts are good for us because they're homemade and use high-quality—organic when possible—ingredients. Whenever I can, I also apply a few tricks to make them even more nutritious: I love sneaking flaxseed and even chia seeds into my batters to provide that extra boost we all need. The first part of this chapter focuses on these simple, healthful breakfasts.

And then there are those *other* mornings, the ones when we have a bit more time on our hands and I can focus on making something special. I hope to help you conquer breakfast by providing a range of flavors and a variety of recipes that will satisfy everyone.

Here's to happy mornings!

Power Coffee

❧ Serves 4

❧ BREW #1:

THE ORIGINAL ❧

4 cups freshly brewed
hot coffee

4 tablespoons (½ stick)
unsalted butter (I like
Kerrygold)

3 to 4 tablespoons natural
cane sugar, such as
turbinado

2 tablespoons liquid
vitamins (optional)

❧ BREW #2:

**THE DAIRY-FREE,
SUGAR-FREE VERSION
(WHEN YOU'RE FEELING
EXTRA HEALTHY) ❧**

4 cups freshly brewed
hot coffee

4 to 6 drops liquid stevia

2 heaping tablespoons
coconut oil

2 tablespoons liquid
vitamins (optional)

❧ Put all the ingredients in a blender. Remove the center plug from the blender lid and hold a towel over the hole to allow steam to escape (or else the lid can blow off from the pressure and send hot coffee flying everywhere!). Blend until smooth and creamy, about 30 seconds. Pour into four mugs. The butter or coconut oil eliminates the need to add any creamer—it's magical.

My father-in-law has four older sisters. We call them the Aunties. They make everyone laugh. Whenever they come visit us in the Bay, they request two things: this coffee... and my Deep-Fried Oreos (page 218). Talk about opposite sides of the spectrum.

It might sound crazy to put butter in coffee, but don't knock it before you try it. It's an amazing way to kick-start the morning. I make two versions—one with butter and one that's dairy-free. Either one gives me (and, apparently, the Aunties) everything I need to conquer the morning—including that all-important energy boost first thing in the morning—and treat my body well from the inside out. I sometimes add a liquid vitamin, like Barlean's The Essential Woman, but I leave that option up to you.

Apple-Cinnamon Oatmeal

⊰ Serves 4

⊰ APPLE COMPOTE ⊱

2 tablespoons
unsalted butter

4 apples, such as
Pink Lady or Honeycrisp,
unpeeled, cored and cut
into ½-inch chunks

½ teaspoon
ground cinnamon

¼ teaspoon
ground nutmeg

¼ cup pure maple syrup

Zest of 1 lemon

Juice of ½ lemon
(about 2 tablespoons)

⊰ OATMEAL ⊱

3½ cups whole milk or
almond milk

2 cups old-fashioned oats

Kosher salt

4 tablespoons
sweetened condensed
milk, for serving

To make the apple compote: Melt the butter in a skillet over medium-high heat. Add the apples, cinnamon, and nutmeg and sauté for 2 minutes. Stir in the maple syrup, lower the heat to medium, and simmer gently until the apples soften, 10 to 12 minutes, stirring occasionally. Stir in the lemon zest and juice and simmer for about 1 minute to combine the flavors. The compote can be made ahead and stored in an airtight container in the refrigerator for up to a week—just warm it up in the microwave before serving.

To make the oatmeal: In a medium saucepan, bring the milk to a boil over high heat. Stir in the oats and a pinch of salt and simmer on low, stirring constantly, until the oats thicken and pull away from the bottom of the pan, 7 to 10 minutes.

For each serving, pour 1 tablespoon of sweetened condensed milk into the bottom of a bowl and add a few heaping scoops of oatmeal. Top it off with warm apple compote.

During fall and winter, I love a warm start to my day that goes beyond my routine cup of coffee. A hearty breakfast always hits the spot, cheering me up when the weather is at its coldest. This oatmeal dish is perfect because it tastes just like apple pie...and who doesn't love apple pie? I sweeten the deal with a little condensed milk. Even better, the apple compote can be prepped ahead and stored in the refrigerator, making breakfast that much easier.

Island Cornmeal Porridge

⤳ Serves 4

¾ cup finely
ground cornmeal

3 cups water

½ cup milk
(preferably whole)

¾ packed cup
dark brown sugar

2 bay leaves

1 teaspoon pure
vanilla extract

¼ teaspoon
ground cinnamon

¼ teaspoon
ground nutmeg

Kosher salt

1 tablespoon
unsalted butter

A handful of raisins,
chopped dates, and/or
chopped toasted
walnuts, for serving

⤳ Put the cornmeal and water in a medium pot and bring to a boil over medium-high heat, stirring often. Lower the heat to medium and cook, stirring frequently, until the cornmeal has thickened, about 5 minutes.

Turn the heat to a low simmer and stir in the milk, brown sugar, bay leaves, vanilla, cinnamon, nutmeg, and a pinch of salt. Simmer, stirring occasionally, until the cornmeal has the consistency of thick oatmeal, about 10 minutes more.

Remove the pot from the heat and remove the bay leaves. Stir in the butter to smooth out the porridge. Let it stand for 5 to 10 minutes before spooning into bowls.

To serve, I like to top each bowl with raisins, dates, and walnuts for sweetness and crunch, but feel free to make it your own by adding your favorite combo of nuts and dried fruits.

When I was a kid, I was not the biggest fan of this porridge. Part of the reason was that we ate it every week at my house. It took moving to LA when I was 17 for me to crave it, making me realize how crazy I was to take my mom's cooking for granted. Spiced and warming, this porridge is my childhood breakfast experience wrapped into one comforting package. Even today when my mom comes to visit the babies (because now that there are grandkids around it's not about visiting me anymore!), I always ask her to make this porridge.

Greek Yogurt Parfaits

Serves 4

1½ cup walnuts,
coarsely chopped

¼ cup raw pumpkin seeds

4 cups plain Greek yogurt
(preferably whole milk)

8 dates, sliced lengthwise
and pitted

2 tablespoons ground
flaxseed

4 tablespoons honey

Preheat the oven to 350°F. Spread the walnuts and pumpkin seeds in a single layer on a rimmed baking sheet and toast until fragrant and lightly golden, about 10 minutes. Let cool slightly.

For serving, you can divide all the ingredients into four bowls any which way you like, ending with the nut mixture sprinkled on top for crunch. But to make a standout parfait, try this: Spoon about ½ cup yogurt in the bottom of four glasses or small mason jars. Take about half of the nut mixture and half of the dates and sprinkle them evenly over each parfait. Top each serving with another ½ cup yogurt. Dividing evenly, sprinkle with the flaxseed and the remaining nut mixture and dates. Drizzle 1 tablespoon of honey over each parfait and serve.

Evvia is a fabulous Greek restaurant in Palo Alto. Whenever I visit, I always end my meal there with their Greek yogurt parfait. This simple breakfast recipe is inspired by that lovely dish. To make it breakfast-ready, I modified it by adding flaxseed and pumpkin seeds. While you can eat it for breakfast, it's also a delicious and healthy anytime snack.

Honey-Pepper Cast-Iron Biscuits

Makes about 12 (2-inch) biscuits

2 cups all-purpose flour

2 tablespoons dark brown sugar

1 tablespoon baking powder

¼ teaspoon baking soda

½ teaspoon kosher salt

¾ cup (1½ sticks) unsalted butter, cold and cubed, plus 1 tablespoon unsalted butter, melted

¼ cup mascarpone cheese

⅔ cup whole milk

½ teaspoon freshly ground black pepper

Honey, for drizzling

Quick Jam (page 20), for serving

Preheat the oven to 450°F. Have a large, well-oiled cast-iron skillet handy.

In a large bowl, whisk together the flour, brown sugar, baking powder, baking soda, and salt. Add the cold butter and use a fork or your hands to squish the butter into the flour until a crumbly mixture forms. When most of the butter has been cut in, add the mascarpone. Using your hands, mix in the mascarpone gently. It will not yet look like dough, and you will have some pea-size pieces of butter. (That will make your biscuits extra flaky.) Pour in the milk and stir with a wooden spoon or rubber spatula until the dough just starts to come together.

Dust a clean surface with flour. Transfer the dough to the surface and pat into a disc about 1 inch thick.

Using a 2-inch round or heart-shaped (my favorite) cookie cutter, or whatever size and shape you like, cut out the biscuits. (Dip the cutter in some flour if your dough is sticking to it.) Gather up any scraps, smoosh them together, and then press the dough into a disc and cut again to make use of all the dough.

Nestle the biscuits in the cast-iron skillet—it's okay for the biscuits to touch each other. Brush the tops with the melted butter and sprinkle with the black pepper. Bake until the tops are golden brown, about 20 minutes. Just remember, if you're using a larger cookie cutter, the biscuits may need more time in the oven.

Let cool for 5 minutes and drizzle honey over the top. Serve warm with jam.

There is something about the combination of pepper and honey that I can't get enough of. (Witness the Honey-Pepper Shrimp on page 122 as more proof.) Those two ingredients turn already great biscuits into something a little more dressed up. I love them with a little bit of jam for breakfast, but they also make great sandwiches, especially with slices of roast pork or country ham dabbed with red pepper jelly. These biscuits are almost like flaky scones, with a little mascarpone mixed in for decadence.

Quick Jam

⤳ Makes 2 to 2½ cups

2 pounds very ripe fruit, such as apricots, figs, or strawberries

1 cup sugar

Juice of 1 lemon (about ¼ cup)

⤳ Remove any stems or pits from the fruit and cut into small, equal-size pieces (leaving the skins on the apricots is fine). If using strawberries, hull and cut into halves or quarters, depending on the size of the berries. Have a pint-size glass jar handy.

In a medium saucepan over medium-high heat, stir together the fruit and sugar. Cook, stirring constantly so the jam does not burn, until the sugar dissolves, about 3 minutes.

Reduce the heat to medium and simmer, stirring occasionally, until the fruit thickens to the consistency of jam, 10 to 15 minutes. (You can test the consistency by dropping a spoonful on a chilled plate to see if it stands up—if it looks runny, cook it a little longer.)

Remove the saucepan from the heat and stir in the lemon juice. Transfer the jam to a glass jar and let it cool to room temperature. Once cool, cap the jar and refrigerate. The jam will keep in the fridge for up to 2 weeks.

While some people like to dedicate a whole day to making jam, I find that it can be just as satisfying to cook up a quick jam with seasonal fruit to keep in the refrigerator. The best time of year to do this is in summer and fall, when so many delicious fruits are available and at their peak freshness. If you're using apricots, add a vanilla bean to the fruit as it simmers for an even sweeter combination. Serve the jam with toast and butter or Honey-Pepper Cast-Iron Biscuits (page 18).

One-Hour Bread

☙ Makes 1 (4-by-8-inch) loaf

3 cups all-purpose flour

1 tablespoon sugar

1 tablespoon instant yeast

1 teaspoon kosher salt

1 cup warm water
(110°F to 115°F)

1 tablespoon unsalted
butter, cut into pieces,
at room temperature

1 large egg, lightly beaten
(optional)

❧ Preheat the oven to 400°F. Lightly oil a 4-by-8-inch loaf pan.

In a stand mixer with the paddle attachment (or simply in a bowl using your hands), combine the flour, sugar, yeast, and salt. With the mixer running on low, slowly pour in the warm water. Mix briefly until the water is absorbed. Remove the paddle, scrape off the excess dough, and attach the dough hook.

Add the butter, turn the mixer to low (or use your hands), and knead the dough until the butter is mixed in and the dough has come together and is smooth and slightly tacky to the touch, about 5 minutes.

Lightly oil a large bowl and put the dough in the bowl. Cover with plastic wrap and let it rest for 15 minutes.

Lightly flour a clean surface and put the dough on top. Divide the dough in half and roll out each piece into a rope slightly longer than 12 inches. Twist the ropes together two or three times. Put the dough in the loaf pan, tucking the ends under. Brush the top of the loaf with the beaten egg (if using).

Bake until the top is golden brown, about 30 minutes. Let the loaf sit in the pan for at least 5 minutes before you turn it out and devour that sucker!

Baking a loaf of bread in an hour sounds impossible—doesn't it have to take all day? Not always, as I discovered with this recipe. I started experimenting with this bread one year when one of my New Year's resolutions was to bake bread every Sunday. The truth is, that resolution didn't last through January. But I still love baking bread, and since this bread takes only an hour, it's not that hard to find the time. This bread is a little denser than a typical sandwich bread, but its chewiness is part of what makes it so addictive. I enjoy it with butter and a little homemade Quick Jam (page 20).

one-hour bread

quick jam

Prosciutto Egg Cups with Asparagus

Serves 4

EGG CUPS

6 very thin prosciutto slices (about 3 ounces)

5 large eggs

½ cup heavy cream

¼ teaspoon kosher salt

¼ teaspoon freshly ground black pepper

6 tablespoons shredded Gruyère cheese

ASPARAGUS

1 tablespoon extra-virgin olive oil

1 bunch asparagus (about 12 ounces), trimmed and cut into 1-inch pieces

1 green onion, thinly sliced, white and light green parts separated from dark green parts

1 cup cherry tomatoes, halved

4 fresh sage leaves, coarsely chopped

Kosher salt

Freshly ground black pepper

To make the egg cups:
Preheat the oven to 400°F. Line a baking sheet with parchment paper or aluminum foil and place a standard-size 12-cup nonstick muffin tin on top.

Line every other cup of the muffin tin with 1 prosciutto slice, pressing the prosciutto snugly into the bottom and up the sides of the cup. There should be some overhang on each side. In a bowl, whisk the eggs and cream until smooth. Season with the salt and pepper.

Divide the egg batter among the prosciutto-lined muffin tin cups, filling each one about three-quarters of the way. Sprinkle each cup with 1 tablespoon shredded cheese and fold the prosciutto over to cover the filling. Bake until bubbly, puffed, and golden brown, about 20 minutes.

To make the asparagus:
When the egg cups are nearly done, heat the oil in a skillet over medium-high heat. Sauté the asparagus until the stalks are lightly browned and have started to soften, 3 to 4 minutes, adding the white and light green parts of the green onion during the last minute of cooking. Turn off the heat and stir in the tomatoes and sage. Season with a pinch each of salt and pepper. Continue to stir with the heat off until everything is mixed well and the tomatoes are warm. Garnish with the dark green onion slices.

Scoop an egg cup (or two) onto each plate, then spoon the asparagus and tomatoes alongside. Serve while still hot.

With salty prosciutto, oozing Gruyère cheese, and creamy eggs served alongside warm asparagus and tomatoes, this is the perfect breakfast crowd pleaser. While this recipe makes six egg cups, I say it serves only four people because someone invariably wants seconds.

Smoked Salmon Scramble

౿ Serves 4

8 large eggs

2 tablespoons heavy
cream

Kosher salt

Freshly ground black pepper

1 tablespoon extra-virgin
olive oil

½ cup supersweet
corn kernels (from
about half a cob)

4 ounces smoked salmon,
cut into strips

½ cup halved
cherry tomatoes

Chopped fresh dill,
for garnish

౿ In a large bowl, whisk together the eggs, cream, and a generous pinch each of salt and pepper.

Heat the oil in a large skillet over medium-low heat. Pour in the eggs and begin to scramble them, gently pushing the eggs around the pan with a spatula, about 1 minute.

Once the eggs are partially cooked, add the corn. Cook for 1 to 2 more minutes until the eggs are nearly done and then fold in the smoked salmon and tomatoes. Remove the pan from the heat and allow the residual heat to warm the salmon and tomatoes through. Sprinkle the dill on top (if desired) and serve.

Smoked salmon and eggs are both great breakfast foods. Put them together and they're even better. I like to dress this dish up a bit with fresh dill—dill and salmon are a natural pairing—and fresh sweet corn, for crunch. If you're feeling frisky, or just so happen to have crème fraîche on hand (just saying...), dab a bit on top.

Ham and Cheese Waffles

Serves 4

1 box Belgian waffle mix, such as Krusteaz, plus any ingredients needed for the mix

3 tablespoons extra-virgin olive oil

1 cup grated Cheddar cheese

½ cup chopped pancetta or ham

Freshly ground black pepper

Plug in a Belgian waffle iron to allow it to preheat (set it to medium-high if you can).

Prepare the waffle batter as directed on the package for 4 servings and pour into a bowl. Stir in the olive oil, Cheddar cheese, pancetta, and black pepper.

When the waffle iron is ready, pour the batter in, close the iron, and cook until the iron indicates that the waffle is done. Repeat with the remaining batter. The recipe makes about 10 squares—about 2½ rounds with the waffle iron. Serve hot.

This recipe is all about thinking outside the box—specifically, a box of Belgian waffle mix. Here's where it gets fancy and wild: I add grated Cheddar and chopped pancetta, pour in a splash of olive oil, and give the batter a few good pinches of freshly cracked pepper. Eat it plain out of the waffle iron and I promise it will be delicious or—my preference—mix a little hot sauce into some maple syrup to serve on the side for dipping.

fancy and wild &

PB&J Cereal French Toast

❄ Serves 4

½ cup peanut butter

½ cup strawberry jam

8 slices hearty white
sandwich bread

2 large eggs

2 tablespoons milk
(preferably whole)

½ teaspoon
ground cinnamon

¼ teaspoon ground
nutmeg

Kosher salt

3 cups sweetened
corn flakes, such as
Frosted Flakes, crushed

4 tablespoons (½ stick)
unsalted butter or
coconut oil

Preheat the oven to 175°F. Put a rimmed baking sheet or platter in the oven to keep the finished French toast warm before serving.

Spread the peanut butter and jelly on the bread to make four sandwiches.

In a wide, shallow bowl, whisk together the eggs, milk, cinnamon, nutmeg, and a pinch of salt. Spread the cereal on a plate or in another shallow bowl.

Dip one sandwich in the egg batter on both sides and shake to drain off the excess. Then coat the battered sandwich thoroughly on both sides with the crushed flakes. Repeat with the remaining three sandwiches.

Melt 2 tablespoons of the butter in a large skillet over medium heat. Working in batches, cook each sandwich on both sides until golden brown on the outside and warm on the inside, about 2 minutes per side, adding more butter and wiping out the pan as needed. If the cereal begins to burn, you may need to lower the heat slightly. Transfer each finished sandwich to the baking sheet in the oven to keep warm.

Cut each sandwich into halves or quarters and enjoy with a giant glass of ice-cold milk. YUM!

This recipe takes your classic peanut butter and jelly sandwich to a whole other level: in the form of French toast. Yes, PB&J can be for breakfast! Unfortunately, peanut butter doesn't always agree with me (the bummer is that my favorite chocolate candy is Reese's Peanut Butter Cups...), so I swap out the peanut butter for almond butter when I have to. Both versions taste fantastic, although I'm still partial to the peanut butter version.

Challah French Toast with Cinnamon Whipped Cream

⊰ Serves 4

⊰ CINNAMON WHIPPED CREAM ⊱

1 cup heavy cream, chilled

1 tablespoon granulated sugar

½ teaspoon ground cinnamon

⊰ FRENCH TOAST ⊱

4 large eggs

¼ cup heavy cream

1 tablespoon dark brown sugar

1 teaspoon pure almond extract

½ teaspoon ground cinnamon

¼ teaspoon ground nutmeg

Kosher salt (optional)

1 loaf challah bread, cut into 1-inch-thick slices

4 tablespoons (½ stick) unsalted butter

Fresh raspberries, for serving

Pure maple syrup, warmed, for serving

To make the cinnamon whipped cream: Combine the cream, sugar, and cinnamon in a bowl and beat with a whisk or an electric mixer until the cream forms soft peaks when the whisk is lifted out of the bowl. (Or use a stand mixer with the whisk attachment—this will make things go much faster, but watch it so you don't overwhip your cream...or you'll have butter on your hands!) Set aside.

To make the French toast: Preheat the oven to 175°F. Put a rimmed baking sheet or platter in the oven to keep the finished French toast warm before serving.

In a wide, shallow bowl, whisk together the eggs, cream, brown sugar, almond extract, cinnamon, nutmeg, and a pinch of salt (if desired).

Dip each slice of challah in the batter on both sides briefly (I do 10 seconds per side so it doesn't get soggy) and shake to drain off the excess.

Melt 2 tablespoons of the butter in a large skillet over medium heat. Working in batches, cook each piece of battered challah on both sides until golden brown on the outside and warm on the inside, about 2 minutes per side, adding more butter and wiping out the pan as needed. Transfer each finished piece to the baking sheet in the oven to keep warm.

Serve with the cinnamon whipped cream, berries, and maple syrup.

I like my French toast sliced thick—this keeps it from getting soggy, and I'm not a soggy French toast girl. But I do like decadence now and again. To make this breakfast stand up tall on the plate, I serve it with a nice dollop of cinnamon whipped cream on top. Buy a pint of heavy cream so you can add a splash to the batter and use most of the rest for the whipped cream.

Pancrepes with Raspberry Sauce

🍂 Serves 4 (or 2 for bigger appetites...)

❧ RASPBERRY SAUCE ❧

1 cup raspberries

¼ cup agave nectar

1 tablespoon freshly squeezed lemon juice

❧ PANCREPES ❧

4 large eggs

2 cups all-purpose flour

1½ cups whole milk

2 tablespoons extra-virgin olive oil

1 tablespoon honey

½ teaspoon pure almond extract

Kosher salt (optional)

Granola, for serving (optional)

❧ To make the raspberry sauce: Combine the raspberries, agave, and lemon juice in a blender and puree. Transfer to a bowl and set aside.

To make the pancrepes: Preheat the oven to 175°F. Put a rimmed baking sheet or platter in the oven to keep the finished pancrepes warm before serving.

In a large bowl, lightly beat the eggs. Whisk in the flour, milk, oil, honey, almond extract, and a pinch of kosher salt (if desired) until smooth. (A few lumps are okay.)

Heat a large nonstick skillet over medium to medium-high heat. Working in batches, pour the batter into the pan to make pancrepes about 5 inches in diameter. Cook the pancrepes for about 2 minutes on each side, then transfer them to the baking sheet in the oven to keep warm. You will have about 12 pancrepes.

To serve, spoon the raspberry sauce on top of the pancrepes and add a handful of granola for crunch, if desired.

Here's the story behind this recipe: I left baking powder out of an ordinary pancake batter because I was all out and thought, what the heck. The result was much better than I expected. It was the perfect textural mix between a pancake and a crepe, tasting like the bottom part of a Dutch baby (which is the best part of a Dutch baby). Now it's become a regular part of our breakfast rotation. I'm hooked on almond extract, so I always add a splash to pancake—and pancrepe—batter.

Breakfast Bread Pudding

⊰ Serves 6 to 8

⊰ BREAD PUDDING ⊱

3 large eggs

1½ cups whole milk, warmed slightly to take the chill off

½ cup honey

2 tablespoons unsalted butter, melted

1 tablespoon pure vanilla extract

2 tablespoons dark brown sugar

Grated zest of 1 orange

1 tablespoon ground cinnamon

½ teaspoon ground nutmeg

¼ teaspoon kosher salt

3½ cups cubed bread, such as challah or brioche, cut into 1-inch pieces

2 Granny Smith apples, cored and cut into ½-inch pieces (optional)

⅓ cup lightly toasted chopped walnuts (optional)

½ cup quick-cooking oats

1 to 2 tablespoons ground flaxseed

⊰ MAPLE-ORANGE GLAZE ⊱

1 tablespoon pure maple syrup

1 tablespoon freshly squeezed orange juice

½ cup confectioners' sugar

To make the bread pudding: Preheat the oven to 375°F. Butter an 8-inch square baking pan or a muffin tin.

In a large bowl, whisk together the eggs, milk, honey, butter, vanilla, brown sugar, orange zest, cinnamon, nutmeg, and salt.

Add the bread cubes and stir until thoroughly combined. Stir in the chopped apple and walnuts if you choose, and then mix in the oats and flaxseed. Pour the mixture into the prepared pan and bake until the top is golden brown and the apples are tender, 45 to 50 minutes in a baking pan, or 25 to 30 minutes for muffins.

To make the maple-orange glaze: Whisk together the maple syrup, orange juice, and confectioners' sugar until creamy and smooth. Drizzle over the bread pudding and serve while the pudding is still warm.

Here's a nice alternative to pancakes. It shows that there is no reason that bread pudding always has to be for dessert (although it does make a delicious dessert, as you'll see on page 210). With a few additions—like apples, walnuts, oats, and flaxseed—bread pudding is ready to conquer mornings around my house. For the best results, use a bread enriched with butter and eggs, such as challah or brioche.

Brown Sugar Bacon

⤳ Serves 4 to 6

10 slices thick-cut bacon

2 tablespoons dark
brown sugar

1 teaspoon freshly ground
black pepper

¼ teaspoon ground
fennel seed

⤳ Preheat the oven to 400°F and place a rack in the center of the oven.

Line a rimmed baking sheet with aluminum foil (for easier cleanup) and put a wire rack on top. Line up the bacon slices side by side on the rack. (It's okay if they touch since they will shrink and separate as they cook.)

In a small bowl, stir together the brown sugar, pepper, and fennel and sprinkle the mixture evenly over the bacon. Bake the bacon until most of the fat has rendered out and the bacon has started to crisp, about 25 minutes. (It will continue to crisp as it cools.) Remove from the oven and allow the bacon to cool to a warm room temperature so that the sugar can harden. Serve.

In my family, this bacon has long been a Sunday morning staple. It all started with a family tradition of going to BrickTops, a local spot in Charlotte, North Carolina, after church. We would roll in at least ten deep—and hungry. While the restaurant makes this bacon to dress up its deviled eggs (and I do like it on my Deviled Eggs—see page 88), we're such fans that each of us requests our own side of bacon without the eggs.

Salty Wheat

The moment I put the spoon to my mouth, I knew it was love. Not because my new husband's attempt at making Cream of Wheat was any good, but because I knew he was hopeless without me.

The endearing part was that Stephen was so certain and confident in the college-made Styrofoam bowl of processed ground "goodness" he presented to me that I didn't have the heart to tell him it was awful—until the next time he made it for me. Filled with salt, salted butter, and lukewarm water heated in the microwave, it was way, way too salty. Top it off with a burned bagel, eggs scrambled to the point of being crispy, and a wonderfully colorful garnish of Fruit Gushers and it was time for some honesty.

Looking back, I'm not sure if it was a ploy to get me cooking or if he really liked his Cream of Wheat that way. Either way, I made sure I was the one doing the cooking from that day on. They say the way to a man's heart is through his stomach. While we all know it's definitely not the *only* way, if you know what I mean, my cooking has brought forth a steady stream of smiles from that man. Truth is I wouldn't have it any other way. It's how I show my love to my whole family, and it's how I am able to express my creativity.

Plus, cooking excitement can be infectious. Eight years later, Stephen learned that he can make a mean pasta with five ingredients, including bell peppers and pancetta (page 158). Although he still does not understand why a red bell pepper is sweet and not spicy. "Then why is it called a pepper?!" He makes a good point. Oh, the mysteries of life.

Here's to no more salty Cream of Wheat!

Cooking with the Littles

IF THERE IS ONE GOLDEN RULE to keep in mind when cooking with kids, it's this: Do not be afraid to make a mess—that's where a lot of the learning happens. And there is so much to gain by getting kids comfortable in the kitchen at an early age. I've found that cooking with my daughter Riley is the best way not only to teach her how to have fun with food but also to inspire her to taste new things. Any mess that is made is easily cleaned up, too.

Setting up the kitchen with a few age-appropriate tools is a good way to start. My sister Maria bought Riley some kid-friendly chef knives that allow her to cut her own apple without me ever having to worry that she'll nick herself by accident. But for the most part, Riley and I are learning as we go. Whatever I'm doing, she can do it with me until we get to the stove. And when we get to the stove, I tell her she can stand with me but behind me so she stays shielded from the flame. Plus she knows she can't touch the adult knives. I also teach cleaning as you go. She can crack the eggs, but she can't then throw the shells on the floor. I don't want to discourage her with a bunch of rules. It's about positive reinforcement, pure and simple. These are the moments that build the memories.

Where to begin? Here are a few ideas:

Make fruit on a stick. ◂ Fruit kebabs are an easy way to get your kids to try a variety of different types of fruit. It's also fun because they can prepare them with you. Try threading cubes of watermelon, mango, apples, and peaches (or other easy-to-cube seasonal fruits) on wooden skewers.

Make pizza. ◂ Store-bought pizza dough—even organic varieties—is getting easier and easier to find. I let Riley shape the dough any which way she likes—sometimes she wants hearts, but always she wants what she wants. Then all you have to do is set out the toppings and let the kids have at it, being on hand to help put the pizza on the baking sheet (lined with parchment paper for easy cleanup) and into the oven. In my family, marinara sauce, pepperoni, sliced mushrooms, and cooked pieces of sausage are always a must for toppings. Riley also likes prosciutto and salami, while I sometimes go green, using pesto as a sauce and topping it afterward with sliced pear and arugula. We sometimes have competitions as to who can come up with the best pizza combos.

Make smoothies. ◂ This is a great way to get kids to eat their greens. I sneak spinach, cucumber, and even kale into smoothies for my family. But I have found the most success when I let Riley put everything in the blender herself. Start with the Island Green Smoothie (page 187) and build from there. When kids have a hand in making it, they are more apt to try it.

Cook with color. ◂ Riley is such a girly girl. She's into all things pink and purple right now...including her food! I sometimes blend fresh strawberries and raspberries into store-bought pancake batter to give it more flavor and a perfectly pink tinge. I let her cut the cooked pancakes into various shapes with cookie cutters.

Make "instant" ice cream. ◀ I slice bananas and freeze them in zip-top bags so they are always handy for making smoothies and, yes, ice cream. Riley and I blend the bananas with a splash of milk—just enough to get the blender going—and season with a pinch of cinnamon and honey. It comes out of the blender looking like decadent soft-serve. Riley can grab a handful of fresh berries and put them on top. Speaking of freezing fruit, frozen grapes make a great treat! They are perfect as a snack on their own, but I like using them as an edible freezer pack for the lunch box. This way, the food in the lunch box stays cool until lunchtime, but there's a built-in healthy snack in there, too.

Here's to kids in the kitchen!

Oven-Baked Chicken Tenders

⁊ Serves 4

4 (4- to 6-ounce) boneless,
skinless chicken breasts

1 cup ground flaxseed
(I like Linwoods brand)

1½ teaspoons flaky
sea salt, such as Maldon

½ teaspoon freshly
ground black pepper

Preheat the oven to
425°F. Line a rimmed baking
sheet with foil and drizzle a
thin layer of oil on top.

Cut each breast lengthwise
into 4 pieces. In a zip-top
bag, combine the flaxseed,
salt, and pepper. Put the
chicken in the bag, seal the
bag, and shake well to coat
the tenders all over.

Put the breaded tenders
on the prepared baking
sheet and bake until cooked
through, 15 to 20 minutes.
It's that simple!

Ground flaxseed makes for a surprisingly crispy—and
healthy!—coating for chicken tenders. What's even better
is this recipe is fun to make with kids: Simply put the chicken
and breading in a zip-top bag, seal the bag, and let the kids
shake it until all the pieces are coated. When buying chicken, I
opt for organic to make it even healthier.

Soft and Chewy
Chocolate Chip Cookies

⤳ Makes 12 large cookies or 24 small cookies

⅓ cup unsalted butter, at room temperature, plus ⅓ cup unsalted butter, melted

1 packed cup dark brown sugar

1 large egg, lightly beaten

1 teaspoon pure vanilla extract

1½ cups all-purpose flour

½ teaspoon baking soda

½ teaspoon kosher salt

2 heaping tablespoons ground flaxseed (optional)

1 cup chocolate chips

Flaky sea salt, such as Maldon (optional)

⤳ Preheat the oven to 375°F. Line two baking sheets with parchment paper or lightly oil them.

In a large bowl, mash together the softened and melted butter. Add the brown sugar and mix well by hand using a spatula. (Or get your kids to do it—you can't go wrong.) Mix in the egg and vanilla, then add the flour, baking soda, salt, and flaxseed (if using). Mix until a crumbly dough forms—it won't look like a smooth cookie batter. Gently mix in the chocolate chips.

Roll the dough into golf ball-size balls and put on the prepared baking sheets, about 6 cookies per sheet, spaced evenly apart. (Or make them smaller and double the yield.)

Bake until the edges just set but the centers are still soft, about 8 minutes. Sprinkle with salt (if desired) and cool completely on the baking sheets.

My baby girl and I love baking together. Although she's not a huge fan of chocolate, I am, and I coerce her into making chocolate chip cookies with me whenever I can. These cookies are soft, perfectly sweet, and packed full of love. I guarantee that you should double the batch if you're going to share. For a more grown-up take, sprinkle flaky sea salt on top as they cool.

Q&A with Riley

A What's your favorite thing to cook with me?

R Fish.

A That's not true.

R Pasta.

A Yes. That's true. What's your favorite thing to bake with me?

R Um...cookies!

A And banana...

R Ummm...

A Banana...

R Bread!

A What do we put in the banana bread?

R Flour. And I don't know what that brown thing is...

A Brown sugar!

R Brown sugarrrrrrrr.

A And we put in chocolate chips.

R Can I put in the chips?

A But you don't like chocolate.

R I want chocolate *white* chips.

A What's your favorite thing to do when we're making pancakes?

R Ummm...

A What is your job? You crack...

R The eggs! [singing] Stirring, stirring, stirring, stirring up my eggs, stirring, stirring, stirring, stirring up my eggs.

A You are my professional egg cracker.

R What—where—how do you make pancakes?

A I put flour, eggs, a little sugar, a little almond extract...

R Can we make a pancake for you?

A Yes.

R What's your favorite thing to cook, Mommy?

A My favorite thing to cook right now is pea soup with scallops. But it always changes.

Winning Lunch

{ SALADS, SOUPS, AND SANDWICHES

I **HAVE TO BE HONEST:** When it comes to sitting down and actually taking the time to eat lunch, I fail—epically! As a work-from-home mom to two little ones, there are weeks when all the days run together. Some days I feel lucky if I find time to eat a banana, and some days I go straight to the drive-through. Let's just say that our days are never boring. And even on days when I do have time to get lunch ready to go, my brain is already on the next task. Sound familiar?

This chapter, a mix of soups, salads, and sandwiches, is part practical...and part wishful thinking. While I know a Spicy Lobster Salad with Avocado Dressing (page 64) is not going to be on the menu every day, it can make for a memorable lunch when I get to spend a rare free afternoon with my closest girlfriends. The same goes for one of my all-time favorite things to cook: Sweet Pea Soup with Herbed Scallops · (page 67).

I find I'm more likely to make time for lunch when it's prepared ahead, and all I have to do is heat it up or assemble it. I love having a few jars of salad dressings on hand for just those occasions.

Make-ahead dishes can also be bigger projects that yield plenty of leftovers, like Meatball and Cabbage Soup (page 71). These leftovers can save the day: Simply reheat for a satisfying lunch.

This chapter has crowd-pleasers, too. When a bunch of family or friends come over (which happens *a lot* at our house), I like to serve Salmon Sandwiches (page 80) and Fragrant Lamb Burgers (page 84), lining them all up on the counter so everyone can take what they want.

Here's to trying for three balanced meals a day!

HOW TO MAKE A QUICK LUNCH SALAD

It's easy—just follow this formula:

Make a dressing + choose lettuce + choose a fruit or veggie + add an extra

Homemade Dressings: Use a few spoonfuls for each serving to suit your preference. When creating salads, keep in mind that Balsamic Dressing is the strongest in flavor and color—when pairing it with fruit, leave out the garlic. The most versatile is the Champagne Dressing, which pairs well with just about anything.

Balsamic Dressing (page 56)	*Citrus Dressing (page 57)*
Champagne Dressing (page 56)	*Creamy Avocado Dressing (page 57)*

Lettuce: Use two handfuls of any of the following for each serving.

Butter lettuce, torn into bite-size pieces	*Romaine, baby leaves or*
Arugula	*torn larger leaves*
Baby spinach	*Spring mix*

Fruits and Veggies: Use about 1 cup total of sliced fruits and/or veggies. Mix and match flavors and textures to find new favorites, like Asian pear and fennel.

Asian pear	*Apple*	*Carrot*
Bosc pear	*Grapefruit*	*Cucumber*
Peach	*Avocado*	*Tomato*
Mango	*Fennel*	

Extras: Use a small handful (no more than 1/2 cup per serving) of any of the following.

Dried cranberries	*Crumbled blue cheese*	*Fennel fronds*
Chopped cooked chicken breast or shrimp	*Grated Pecorino Romano cheese*	*Croutons*
Toasted walnuts or almonds	*Fresh flat-leaf parsley leaves*	*Crushed crackers*

HOMEMADE DRESSINGS

I use Mason jars to store these dressings so it's easy to always have homemade dressings on hand—just shake them up and they're ready to go. If the oil in the dressing solidifies in the refrigerator, just leave the jar out at room temperature for a few minutes.

Balsamic Dressing

1 garlic clove, minced

¼ teaspoon kosher salt

¼ cup balsamic vinegar

1 cup extra-virgin olive oil

Freshly ground
black pepper

ᕽ In a small bowl, mash the garlic with the salt (this takes away some of the sting of the raw garlic). Transfer to a mason jar. Pour in the vinegar and olive oil and season with pepper to taste. Cap with a lid and shake before using.

Champagne Dressing

1 tablespoon
minced shallot

¼ cup champagne vinegar
or red wine vinegar

¼ teaspoon kosher salt

Dark brown sugar

1 cup extra-virgin olive oil

Freshly ground
black pepper

ᕽ Combine the shallot, vinegar, salt, and a pinch of brown sugar in a mason jar and let sit for 5 minutes. (This helps remove the raw flavor from the shallot.) Add the olive oil and a pinch of pepper. Cap with a lid and shake before using.

Citrus Dressing

1 lemon, halved

¼ teaspoon kosher salt

¼ teaspoon sugar

1 cup extra-virgin olive oil

⌾ Mince one lemon half (including the rind). Remove any seeds. Transfer to a mason jar. Squeeze the remaining lemon half into the jar (discard the spent lemon half). Add the salt and sugar and pour in the olive oil. Cap with a lid and shake before using.

Creamy Avocado Dressing

6 tablespoons freshly squeezed lime juice

¼ cup water

¼ cup rice wine vinegar

¼ cup honey

1 avocado, peeled, pitted, and cut into chunks

1 small shallot, minced

1 serrano pepper, seeded and minced

½ teaspoon kosher salt, or more to taste

Freshly ground black pepper

⌾ Combine all the ingredients in a blender and blend until smooth. Taste, seasoning with more salt and pepper if desired. This dressing is best served fresh, but in a pinch it can be stored in the refrigerator for up to 1 day.

Pear and Arugula Salad with Shaved Parmesan

↝ Serves 4

¾ cup toasted walnuts

¼ cup plus 1 tablespoon extra-virgin olive oil

Leaves from 2 thyme sprigs

Kosher salt

1½ tablespoons freshly squeezed lemon juice

Freshly ground black pepper

5 ounces arugula

1 pear (preferably Bosc), cored and thinly sliced

1 block Parmesan, for shaving over the salad

⁂ In a small bowl, mix the toasted walnuts with 1 tablespoon of the olive oil, the thyme leaves, and a good pinch of salt.

In a large salad bowl, whisk together the remaining ¼ cup olive oil and the lemon juice. Season with salt and pepper to taste. Add the arugula and pear and toss until evenly coated. Mix in the seasoned walnuts. Using a vegetable peeler, shave as many or as few strips of Parmesan over the salad as you'd like. Serve immediately.

I know, I know, arugula salad sounds so boring. But with the right ingredients—some toasted walnuts, fresh herbs, really good olive oil—you won't believe how quickly everyone will come back for seconds. I'm a big fan of Bosc pears in salads; they seem to keep their crunch better than other varieties. You can easily convert this into a citrus arugula salad with some grapefruit segments and sliced fennel in place of the pear. You also can use the Champagne Dressing (page 56) or the Citrus Dressing (page 57) in place of the olive oil and lemon juice used here.

Toasting nuts before adding them to salads makes a big difference in flavor. The best way to toast walnuts is gently—high heat only chars the outside, while the inside stays raw. To toast walnuts for this salad, scatter them on a rimmed baking sheet and bake at 350°F until evenly golden brown, 15 to 20 minutes. You can test a nut by breaking it in half and seeing if the inside is lightly golden.

Quinoa-Broccolini Salad

⊰ Serves 2 to 4

⊰ SALAD ⊱

1 cup quinoa

1²/₃ cups water, plus more for rinsing

Kosher salt

1 bunch broccolini, trimmed

Freshly ground black pepper

2 tablespoons extra-virgin olive oil

1 cooked chicken breast, chopped (optional)

⊰ DRESSING ⊱

2 tablespoons minced shallot

1 garlic clove, minced

2 tablespoons freshly squeezed lemon juice

2 tablespoons red wine vinegar

1 tablespoon honey

¼ teaspoon dried chile flakes

Kosher salt

⅓ cup chopped raisins

¼ cup extra-virgin olive oil

To make the salad: Preheat the oven to 425°F. Line a rimmed baking sheet with aluminum foil.

Put the quinoa in a fine-mesh strainer and rinse well. Transfer the quinoa to a saucepan and add 1²/₃ cups fresh water. Add a pinch of salt and bring to a simmer, then cover and cook until most of the water has absorbed into the grain, about 15 minutes. Let stand, covered, for 15 additional minutes to steam.

Meanwhile, scatter the broccolini on the foil-lined baking sheet. Season with salt and pepper and drizzle the oil over the top. Rub the seasonings and oil into the broccolini. Roast until the florets are nicely browned and the stalks have started to become tender but are still firm when pierced with a fork, about 10 minutes. Let cool to room temperature, then coarsely chop.

To make the dressing: In a large bowl, mix the shallot, garlic, lemon juice, vinegar, honey, and chile flakes. Season with a few pinches of salt. Stir in the raisins and let sit for 5 minutes. Whisk in the oil.

Add the quinoa and broccolini to the dressing and mix to coat well. Season with salt to taste. Fold in the chicken (if using) and serve at room temperature, or cover and refrigerate for up to 3 days and serve chilled, adding lemon juice or salt as needed to refresh the flavors.

Quinoa is one of those foods that always make you feel good after you've eaten it. So is broccolini. The two go great together with the right combination of seasonings and textures. Having this power salad in the refrigerator can help conquer the daily "what's for lunch" challenge.

Ridiculously Easy Carrot Salad

❧ Serves 4

3 large carrots, peeled and shredded (about 2 cups)

1 pint cherry tomatoes, halved

1 avocado, peeled, pitted, and cut into chunks

Kosher salt

Freshly ground black pepper

Juice of 1 lemon (about ¼ cup)

In a bowl, toss together the carrots, tomatoes, and avocado chunks. Season with a few generous pinches of salt and pepper. Pour the lemon juice over and mix to evenly coat. Serve immediately.

This salad is so easy to make, but it tastes so good—even my kids love it! It's all about light flavors, with the avocado (instead of oil) providing a bit of richness. I like it on its own, but it's also good with some chopped cooked shrimp mixed in for some protein. To shred the carrots, use the medium holes on a box grater or the shredding attachment on a food processor.

Spicy Lobster Salad with Avocado Dressing

❧ Serves 4

2 fresh lobster tails in the shell (about 10 ounces each)

2 tablespoons unsalted butter

1 to 1½ teaspoons Old Bay Seasoning

½ fennel bulb, plus fronds for garnish

1 Asian pear, cored and thinly sliced

1 cup finely diced jicama

5 ounces arugula

Kosher salt

1 cup Creamy Avocado Dressing (page 57)

❧ Place one lobster tail on a cutting board with the top hard shell facing up. Use kitchen shears to cut through the center of the first two segments of the shell. Turn the tail over and cut along one side of the bottom shell until you reach the bottom of the tail. Gently pry the shell open and pull out the tail meat. You may need to cut the very base of the tail meat to remove it from the bottom.

Using a knife, make a shallow cut down the back of the tail meat and remove the vein. Cut the tail crosswise into slices about ¼ inch thick. Repeat with second lobster tail.

Melt the butter in a skillet over medium-high heat. Add the lobster, season with Old Bay, and sauté, tossing occasionally, until lightly golden,

about 5 minutes. Do not overcook the lobster—take the pan off the heat when the lobster meat still looks just slightly undercooked, as the carryover heat in the pan will allow it to continue to cook. Taste, adding a bit more Old Bay if desired.

Cut out the core of the fennel bulb half. Using a sharp knife, cut the fennel into super thin slices. (If you happen to have a mandoline, use it instead for even thinner slices.)

In a bowl, toss together the fennel, pear, jicama, and arugula with a pinch of salt and a few generous spoonfuls of the dressing. Divide the salad among four plates and top with the lobster. Drizzle a little more dressing over the top. Garnish with the fennel fronds and serve immediately.

This salad is what I immediately think of when I want something sophisticated but also light and fresh—especially on those rare days I get to spend with my girlfriends. There's crunch, spice, and sweetness, all with a luxe edge. If this salad is wrong, I don't want to be right! If lobster tails are hard to come by, try making this dish with scallops, crab, or shrimp. The avocado dressing complements all equally well.

Sweet Pea Soup with Herbed Scallops

⊰ Serves 4

⊰ SOUP ⊱

1 tablespoon extra-virgin olive oil

1 medium shallot, minced

2 garlic cloves, coarsely chopped

1 (16-ounce) bag frozen peas

Kosher salt

Freshly ground black pepper

1½ cups heavy cream

2 packed cups baby spinach leaves (about 3 ounces)

1 green onion, thinly sliced, for garnish

Grated zest and juice of 1 lemon, for garnish

⊰ SCALLOPS ⊱

2 tablespoons unsalted butter, at room temperature

1 garlic clove, minced

1 teaspoon minced green onion

1 teaspoon minced fresh flat-leaf parsley

1 pound large dry-packed scallops (8 to 12 scallops), side muscles removed

Kosher salt

Freshly ground black pepper

1 tablespoon canola oil

To make the soup:

Heat the oil in a medium saucepan over medium heat. Sauté the shallot and garlic until the shallot has softened and the garlic has started to turn golden, about 2 minutes.

Pour in the peas and cook, stirring occasionally, to let the peas thaw out, about 5 minutes. Add a generous pinch each of salt and pepper. Pour in the heavy cream and cook just until the cream starts to simmer—do not let it boil.

continued on page 68 ⌒

When Stephen hits a crazy-good shot, he gets this amazing feeling. That's how I feel when I make a dish that comes together so perfectly that I can't wait to make it again. A sweet pea soup with beautiful scallops—what more could I want? When buying scallops, look for dry-packed scallops, which will caramelize in the pan better than wet-packed scallops. Even more importantly, dry-packed scallops taste a lot better than scallops that have been pumped with water (and who knows what chemical additives). Scallops are a cinch to prepare; just use a paring knife to pull off the small side muscle that attaches the scallop to its shell. Here I've made a simple garlic and herb butter, but you can cut out that step and buy an already prepared flavored butter (Kerrygold makes a good one).

Sweet Pea Soup with Herbed Scallops, continued

Put the spinach in the jar of a blender and pour the soup over it. Blend until smooth, and season with more salt and pepper to taste. Pour the soup back into the pan and keep warm over medium-low heat. Have four warm soup bowls ready.

To make the scallops: In a small bowl, mash together the butter, garlic, green onion, and parsley with a spoon.

Pat the scallops dry with a paper towel and season with salt and pepper.

Heat the canola oil in a large skillet over medium-high heat. Sear the scallops on one side until deep golden brown, about 2 minutes (for the best sear, avoid the temptation to move the scallops around). Flip the scallops and add the garlic-herb butter to the pan, gently shaking and tilting the pan to melt the butter and coat the scallops. Sear the scallops on the second side for only 1 to 2 minutes; avoid overcooking. Remove the scallops from the pan and keep warm.

Bring the soup to a simmer briefly, just to ensure it's hot. Ladle the soup into the warmed bowls. Place the scallops on top and garnish the scallops with sliced green onion, a bit of lemon zest, and a squeeze of lemon juice. Serve immediately.

Cauliflower and Leek Soup with Crispy Pancetta

⁂ Serves 4 to 6

3 large leeks (about 2 pounds)

2 ounces pancetta, cut into thin strips

3 tablespoons unsalted butter

2 garlic cloves, coarsely chopped

1 teaspoon kosher salt, plus more to taste

½ teaspoon ground white pepper or freshly ground black pepper, plus more to taste

2 tablespoons all-purpose flour

1 cup dry white wine

5 cups water or vegetable broth

1 head cauliflower, broken into florets (about 4 cups)

½ cup heavy cream

½ cup grated Pecorino Romano cheese

To clean the leeks, lop off the dark green ends and put them in the compost heap. Cut each leek in half lengthwise almost to the root and wash under running water, fanning the layers open to help remove any grit. Shake the leek free of water and slice crosswise. You will have about 8 cups of sliced leeks.

Heat a large pot over medium heat. Add the pancetta and cook until crispy, about 3 minutes. Drain the pancetta on paper towels.

Discard all but 1 tablespoon of the pancetta fat and add the butter. Raise the heat to medium-high. Add the leeks and sauté until they begin to soften and wilt (but before they start to brown), about 3 minutes. Add the garlic and cook for 1 minute longer. Season with the salt and pepper.

Stir in the flour to coat the leeks and cook until the flour begins to turn golden, about 2 minutes. Pour in the wine and cook for 1 minute, scraping any bits of flour off the bottom of the pot. Pour in the water and stir until the flour is well incorporated.

continued on page 70

Cauliflower and leeks are available year round, but they're especially welcome when you want warm food on a chilly day. Leeks have a much gentler flavor than regular onions, and cauliflower is like broccoli's sweeter, milder sister. The two come together as an unbeatable duo in this creamy, rich soup. For a crunchy topping, I cook pancetta until crisp, then I set it aside and use the fat for cooking the leeks. Then, to make the soup extra creamy, I puree it in a blender. It makes a big pot, so plan on blending the soup in batches.

Cauliflower and Leek Soup with Crispy Pancetta, continued

Add the cauliflower and bring the liquid to a boil. Reduce the heat to medium-low and gently simmer until the cauliflower is tender, about 20 minutes.

Transfer half of the soup to a blender and add half of the cream and half of the cheese. Remove the center plug from the blender lid and hold a towel over the hole to allow steam to escape (or else the lid can blow off from the pressure and send hot soup flying everywhere!). Blend until smooth and season with more salt and pepper to taste. Repeat with the remaining soup, blending it with the remaining cream and cheese. Pour both blended batches back into the pot and gently heat. Ladle into serving bowls, top with crispy pancetta, and serve.

Meatball and Cabbage Soup

✌ Serves 8 to 10

✦ MEATBALLS ✦

2 pounds ground turkey

1 cup uncooked white rice
(long grain or jasmine)

½ cup finely diced
yellow onion

2 large eggs, lightly beaten

2 tablespoons
Worcestershire sauce

2 teaspoons kosher salt

1 teaspoon freshly ground
black pepper

1 teaspoon ground cumin

¼ cup chopped
fresh cilantro

✦ SOUP ✦

3 tablespoons extra-virgin
olive oil

½ cup finely diced
yellow onion

3 garlic cloves, minced

2 tablespoons
chili powder

1 teaspoon dried oregano

1 teaspoon kosher salt

Freshly ground
black pepper

1 (6-ounce) can
tomato paste

½ cup ketchup

1 (28-ounce) can whole
tomatoes, including liquid

½ small head cabbage,
cored and shredded
(about 4 cups)

4 cups chicken or
beef broth

2 cups water

✦ SERVING ✦

Grated Monterey Jack or
Cheddar cheese

Diced avocado

Lime wedges

Tortilla chips

To make the meatballs:
Preheat the oven to 425°F.
Line a baking sheet with
aluminum foil and lightly
coat with a nonstick
cooking spray.

Combine all the meatball
ingredients in a large bowl
and mix well. (Use your
hands, people!)

Form the mixture into about
36 golf ball–size balls and
place on the prepared baking sheet.

Roast the meatballs until
they are firm and just beginning to brown on top, about
20 minutes. It's okay if they
are not cooked through, as
they will continue to cook
in the soup later. (Heads up!
When roasting, these meatballs sometimes form a layer

continued on page 72 ↪

I magine the sound of rain on the windowpane. (Yes, I like a corny rhyme from time to time.)
A fire roaring in the fireplace. What's missing? This soup, which is a southwestern version of
cabbage soup. It's unusual in that the meatballs are formed with ground turkey mixed with
uncooked rice and eggs. This makes them more delicate than meatballs mixed with breadcrumbs, so I roast them in the oven before putting them in the soup to help them stay together.

Meatball and Cabbage Soup, continued

of goo around them. Don't worry—it's just coagulated proteins. Once the meatballs are cool enough to touch, simply lift each one off of the sheet and drain the excess oil on a paper towel. I promise this soup looks terrific when it's finished.)

To make the soup: Heat the oil in a large pot or Dutch oven over medium heat. Add the onion and sauté until it begins to soften (but before it starts to brown), about 3 minutes. Add the garlic, chili powder, and oregano and cook, stirring, for 1 minute longer. Season with the salt and a pinch of pepper.

Stir in the tomato paste, cooking briefly until the paste begins to turn brick red. Pour in the ketchup and the canned tomatoes with their juice and bring to a brisk simmer. Cook over medium heat until the tomatoes have thickened a bit, about 5 minutes. To smooth out the soup, blend with an immersion blender on low for about 30 seconds to break up the tomatoes. Alternatively, crush the tomatoes with a spoon or potato masher as they cook.

Add the cabbage, broth, and water and bring to a boil. Add the meatballs and simmer over medium-low heat until the meatballs are cooked through and tender, about 25 minutes. (This also gives the rice enough time to cook.) The soup should be thick enough to lightly coat the back of a spoon but not as thick as a stew. If it's too thick, stir in more water.

To serve: Ladle the soup into bowls. Top with grated cheese and diced avocado and offer lime wedges and tortilla chips alongside.

Mom's Leftover Chicken Soup

᪣ Serves 4

1 large leek

1½ to 2 cups peeled and diced butternut squash

2 large celery stalks, diced

½ yellow onion, diced

2 thyme sprigs

1 oregano sprig

2 bay leaves

A few handfuls of shredded cooked chicken or turkey (use however much you have)

Kosher salt

Freshly ground black pepper

4 cups chicken or vegetable broth

4 cups water

½ cup dry white wine

᪣ To clean the leek, lop off the dark green end and put it in the compost heap. Cut the leek in half lengthwise almost to the root and wash under running water, fanning the layers open to help remove any grit. Shake the leek free of water and slice crosswise.

Combine the leek, butternut squash, celery, onion, thyme, oregano, and bay leaves in a large stockpot. Add the chicken and season with a pinch each of salt and pepper. Pour in the broth, water, and wine and bring to a boil. Lower to a simmer and cook, stirring occasionally, until the squash is tender when pierced with a fork, 15 to 20 minutes. Remove the herb sprigs and bay leaves. Taste the soup and season with more salt and pepper as needed. Ladle into bowls and serve.

I should call this *Mom's Leftover Chicken* or *Turkey Soup*, because although it's a good way to use up what's left from a roast chicken, it's also perfect for the day after Thanksgiving or Christmas when there is leftover turkey to be dealt with. These flavors—celery, butternut squash, leek, thyme—are so classic and familiar, but the best part is how easy this soup is to make: Simply combine all the ingredients in a stockpot and simmer until the squash is fork-tender.

You can take one extra step if you choose: Because my mom's family is from Jamaica, we love adding dumplings to everything, including this soup. You can add the fried dumplings on page 147, or you can make simple boiled dumplings. Here's how: When the soup is simmering, mix 1 cup all-purpose flour with ⅓ cup water to form a dough. Roll the dough into little balls with the palms of your hands, then drop them into the soup during the last 5 minutes or so. You'll have about 24 dumplings. Make 'em or leave 'em out—it's totally up to you!

Carolina Chowder

❧ Serves 6 to 8

4 tablespoons (½ stick) unsalted butter

2 cups fresh or frozen (and thawed) sweet corn kernels

1 cup chopped fennel, reserving any fennel fronds for garnish

2 shallots, minced

2 tablespoons all-purpose flour

Kosher salt

Freshly ground black pepper

3 cups fish stock or clam stock (or vegetable broth in a pinch)

2 cups whole milk

2 cups heavy cream

3 large red-skinned potatoes, scrubbed and diced (about 1¼ pounds)

1 pound crabmeat, picked through to make sure no shells remain

¼ teaspoon garlic powder

Cream sherry, for serving (optional)

❧ In a large heavy-bottomed pot or Dutch oven, melt the butter over medium heat. Add the corn, fennel, and shallot and cook, stirring occasionally, until softened, about 3 minutes. Sprinkle the flour on top and cook until barely golden (you want to create a really light roux), about 2 minutes. Season with a pinch or two each of salt and pepper.

Pour in the fish stock, milk, and cream and bring to a boil. Lower to a simmer and cook, stirring often, until the soup starts to thicken, about 10 minutes. Add the potatoes and cook until they are fork-tender, another 10 to 15 minutes. Stir in the crab and garlic powder and simmer for a few minutes more to bring the flavors together.

To serve, spoon 1 teaspoon of cream sherry into each bowl, if desired. Ladle the soup on top, making sure to give everyone equal quantities of crab and potato. Top with fennel fronds if desired. Serve immediately.

Steps away from my in-laws' house in Charlotte is a place called Red Rocks Café. We have gone there countless times for family meals. The one thing we always get is the she-crab soup, a rich soup similar to clam chowder but made with (obviously) crab. I love it, but what can I say—crustaceans are my jam. I've since created my own version, adding corn, potatoes, and shallots. This soup makes a big pot and is best for days when you're expecting friends over. (It doesn't freeze well.) I know people from the coasts can get loyal to Dungeness or blue crab, so use whatever crab you like best. Also keep an eye out for fish stock at the store—Bar Harbor is a reliable brand. I like to serve this soup with a touch of cream sherry in each bowl—be sure to use sweet cream sherry, not dry sherry, and certainly not cooking sherry!

crustaceans are my jam ℒ

Sweet Chili Shrimp Wraps

⅋ Serves 4 to 6

⁂ JICAMA SALAD ⁂

1 cup peeled and finely diced jicama

1 serrano pepper, seeded (if desired, for less heat) and minced

2 tablespoons freshly squeezed lime juice

2 teaspoons rice wine vinegar

Kosher salt

Freshly ground black pepper

⁂ SHRIMP ⁂

½ cup mayonnaise

½ cup sweet chili sauce, such as Thai Kitchen or Mae Ploy

Canola oil, for frying

2 pounds jumbo shrimp (21 to 25 per pound), peeled and deveined (see page 124)

1 teaspoon kosher salt

2 tablespoons cornstarch

⁂ SERVING ⁂

2 green onions, thinly sliced

Butter lettuce, for serving

⁂ To make the jicama salad: In a medium bowl, toss together the jicama, serrano pepper, lime juice, and rice wine vinegar and season with a pinch or so each of salt and pepper. Let the salad sit at room temperature so the flavors meld while you make the shrimp.

To make the shrimp: In a bowl large enough to hold the cooked shrimp and the jicama salad, stir together the mayonnaise and chili sauce. Set aside.

In a 4-quart saucepan or Dutch oven, heat 1 inch of oil (about 3 cups oil, depending on the pan). Line a plate with paper towels and have a slotted spoon handy. To test if the oil is hot enough, put the end of a wooden spoon in the oil and see if bubbles form around it. (The ideal oil temperature is 350°F; feel free to check it with a deep-fry thermometer.)

Put the shrimp in a bowl and season with the salt. Sprinkle with the cornstarch and toss to coat the shrimp evenly. Working in batches to avoid crowding the pan, fry the shrimp, using a slotted spoon to keep them from sticking together, until pink and opaque and lightly crisp, 1 to 2 minutes. Using the slotted spoon, transfer the shrimp to the paper towel-lined plate to drain off excess oil. Repeat with the remaining shrimp.

While still hot, transfer the shrimp to the bowl with the mayo-chili sauce and stir to coat. Add the jicama salad and mix it all together.

Sprinkle the green onions on top. Serve with the lettuce leaves to make wraps or cups or, if you prefer, alongside hot rice.

This is my take on the chicken lettuce wraps served at some well-known chain restaurants around the country. I always notice that the lettuce never actually works as a wrap, so it's more of a cup. The combination of different textures—from the soft butter lettuce leaves to the crunch of the jicama salad—is so much fun, though, who cares if it's not a "real" wrap? My version features an addictively sweet and spicy shrimp. If you want to include more greens—and to increase the strength of the wrap/cup—double up on the lettuce leaves.

Salmon Sandwiches with Mango and Asian Pear Salad

⊰ Serves 4

FRUIT SALAD

2 cups diced mango

2 Asian pears, peeled, cored, and diced

2 tablespoons honey

1 teaspoon chili oil

Small handful of fresh mint leaves, chopped

Kosher salt

SALMON SANDWICHES

4 (4- to 6-ounce) salmon fillets

Coarse sea salt

Freshly ground black pepper

1 teaspoon paprika

4 lemon wedges

4 tablespoons (½ stick) unsalted butter, at room temperature

1 tablespoon minced garlic

½ cup plain whole-milk Greek yogurt

¼ cup finely chopped fresh basil

4 brioche buns, split

Handful of arugula

To make the fruit salad: In a large bowl, toss together the mango, pear, honey, chili oil, mint, and a pinch of salt. (You can do this an hour or two in advance; cover the bowl and refrigerate it until ready to serve.)

To make the salmon sandwiches: Preheat the oven to 425°F. Line a rimmed baking sheet with aluminum foil and oil it lightly.

Place the salmon fillets on the baking sheet. Season each fillet with a generous pinch each of salt and pepper and ¼ teaspoon paprika. Bake until the salmon flakes easily when pierced with a fork, about 8 minutes. Squeeze a lemon wedge over each fillet.

Meanwhile, in a small bowl, stir together the butter and garlic. In a separate small bowl, stir together the yogurt and basil.

Spread the garlic butter onto both cut sides of each bun. Lightly toast the buns, butter-side down, in a sauté pan over medium heat until golden brown, 1 to 2 minutes.

Spread the basil-yogurt spread on the toasted sides of the buns. Put a piece of salmon and some arugula on the bottom half of each bun and then put the top half on. Spear each sandwich with a knife (if going all out with presentation) and dig in, with the fruit salad served alongside.

When a lot of family comes over for lunch, I set up an assembly line to put these sandwiches together before lining them up on a big wooden chopping block. To hold the sandwiches together (and because it looks cool), I stab each sandwich with a steak knife. You don't have to make the salad, but the flavors complement the salmon perfectly, and it's so pretty. One more pointer: If you happen to have any Brown Sugar Bacon (page 38) left over from breakfast, it will put these sandwiches over the top.

Red Wine–Braised Onions

I consider these caramelized onions a must-have topping for all burgers and steaks (try them with my Easy Pan Steaks on page 153). They're not hard to make, and you can prepare them up to 3 days ahead of time and store them in an airtight container in the refrigerator. Simply reheat in the microwave or in a covered skillet over low heat.

Here's how to do it: Heat 1 tablespoon extra-virgin olive oil in a saucepan over medium heat. Add 2 cups thinly sliced red onions to the pan and cook until the onions are wilted, about 4 minutes. Add ½ cup dry red wine, 1 teaspoon sugar, and a pinch of kosher salt. Continue to cook the onions until they start to soften, then lower the heat to medium-low and cook gently until the onions have soaked up all the liquid and have started to caramelize, about 15 minutes. You can add some sliced cremini mushrooms for even more flavor.

Fragrant Lamb Burgers

⁂ Serves 4

1 pound ground lamb

2 tablespoons minced shallot (about 1 small shallot)

¼ cup chopped fresh flat-leaf parsley

Grated zest of 1 lemon

1¼ teaspoons kosher salt

½ teaspoon freshly ground black pepper

1 teaspoon garlic powder

½ teaspoon onion powder

½ teaspoon ground cumin

¼ cup crumbled Gorgonzola cheese

1 tablespoon extra-virgin olive oil

Basil-yogurt spread (see page 80; optional)

4 pretzel rolls, split and lightly toasted

Red wine–braised onions (see sidebar page 81)

4 beefsteak tomatoes, cut into thick slices

4 to 8 large butter lettuce leaves

⁂ In a large bowl, combine the lamb, shallot, parsley, zest, salt, pepper, garlic powder, onion powder, and cumin. (Use your hands to mix well!) Mix in the Gorgonzola briefly to combine. Shape the mixture into four patties about 4 inches in diameter.

Heat the olive oil in a large skillet over medium heat. Cook the patties for 4 minutes per side for medium or until cooked to your liking. (I like these burgers with a pink center.)

If desired, spread the basil-yogurt spread on the cut sides of each roll. Place a burger on the bottom half of each roll and top with caramelized onions, tomatoes, lettuce, and anything else you like, then put the top half of the roll on. Spear the sandwich with a knife (if going all out with presentation) and dig in.

When I make these burgers, I usually line them up next to the Salmon Sandwiches (page 80) on a heavy wooden cutting board. That way everyone can come up to the counter and help themselves—cutting them in half if need be...but usually this doesn't happen. These burgers get their name from the aromatic cumin, garlic powder, and Gorgonzola that I mix into the meat—and also from the delicious caramelized red onions on top. You can use any buns you like to make these burgers, but my favorite lately is pretzel rolls. If some of your friends like to go traditional with lamb, leave a jar of mint jelly on the counter so they can help themselves.

Game Day or Snack Time

Let's face it: If you are having a crowd over on game day, it can be chaos. I can't tell you how many times my husband has invited guests over and given me little to no notice! But I learned long ago not to panic when we have a last-minute party. I can always figure out how to put something together so my lovely guests won't go hungry. That's really what this chapter is about: finger foods that are perfect for parties and family get-togethers. I should just call them "conversation eats."

I also believe in working ahead. When you throw a game day party, you want to be able to enjoy everyone's company and not stay holed up in the kitchen. Planning dishes that can be prepared ahead—even the night before—makes this easy to do. The one exception to the finger-food rule in this chapter is my Game Day Pasta (page 100). In my family, game days can also be working days. For us, this pasta is an essential carbo-loading meal.

Let's talk game plan: The Sticky Honey-Garlic Baby Back Ribs (page 104) are awesome when made the night before. Dips like Red Pepper Hummus (page 93) also can be made a day (or even two) ahead. A few snacks—like Cheesy Guacamole (page 91), Island Ahi Tuna (page 99), and Deviled Eggs (page 88)—are best the day they are made, but they can still be put together an hour or so before the first guest rings the doorbell.

Have no fear; the snacks are here. Here's to keeping the momentum going!

Deviled Eggs

◦﹥ Serves 6

6 large eggs

Scant ¼ cup Miracle Whip

2 tablespoons minced fresh chives

1 teaspoon minced shallot

1 teaspoon sweet pickle relish, or more to taste

¼ teaspoon kosher salt, or more to taste

¼ teaspoon freshly ground black pepper, or more to taste

1 slice Brown Sugar Bacon (page 38), cut into small squares or strips

◦﹥ Put the eggs in a single layer in a medium saucepan and cover with cool water. Bring the water to a boil, then cover, turn off the heat, and let the eggs sit in the hot water for 11 minutes. Meanwhile, fill a bowl with ice and cold water.

After 11 minutes, transfer the eggs to the ice water to stop the cooking. When completely cold, peel the eggs.

Cut the eggs in half lengthwise. Scoop out the yolks and put them in a small bowl. Mash the yolks well with a fork to break up the pieces. (For a smoother consistency, you can push the yolks through a mesh strainer instead.) Mix in the Miracle Whip, chives, shallot, relish, salt, and pepper. Taste, adjusting the seasoning with more salt, pepper, relish, or whatever you desire.

Divide the yolk mixture among the egg white halves, filling the holes with heaping spoonfuls. To finish, spear a piece of bacon into the center of each deviled egg. Serve immediately or refrigerate and serve within 4 hours.

Some may think it's a travesty, but I use Miracle Whip in my deviled egg filling—it helps me achieve that perfect balance of sweet and savory. I also like to add a little minced shallot and chives, as well as a spoonful of sweet relish. Don't forget the Brown Sugar Bacon (page 38)! Don't skip this step—the recipe isn't the same without it. Everything is better with bacon.

A note on prep: Slightly older eggs peel more easily than fresher ones. If you have the time to plan ahead, buy eggs and keep them in the refrigerator for a week or two before hard-boiling them.

Prosciutto-Wrapped Dates

❧ Serves 4 to 6

12 dates, cut in half lengthwise and pitted

About ⅓ cup crumbled Gorgonzola cheese

Freshly ground black pepper

6 very thin prosciutto slices, cut in half lengthwise, kept cold until needed

※ Preheat the oven to 450°F.

Fill each date half with cheese. Sprinkle pepper on top of the cheese, then put both halves back together and wrap with prosciutto.

Place the stuffed and wrapped dates on a rimmed baking sheet.

Bake until the cheese has melted and the prosciutto is lightly caramelized, 8 to 10 minutes. Serve warm.

For my 25th birthday, we went to Tyler Florence's restaurant El Paseo in Mill Valley. He served us these bacon-wrapped dates, and afterward I started craving them all the time. Now I order bacon-wrapped dates nearly every time I see them on a menu. In this homemade version, I fill the dates with Gorgonzola, and I swapped out bacon for prosciutto, which is much easier to roll around the dates. Keep the prosciutto chilled before you roll! It makes the job a snap.

Cheesy Guacamole with Homemade Pita Chips

☙ Serves 8

❧ PITA CHIPS ❧

6 large pita pockets

¼ cup extra-virgin olive oil, for brushing

Spike Vege-Sal Magic! or kosher salt

❧ GUACAMOLE ❧

4 ripe Hass avocados

½ cup grated Havarti cheese

¼ cup finely chopped red onion

2 teaspoons minced garlic

Juice of 1 lime (about 3 tablespoons)

Kosher salt

Freshly ground black pepper

2 tablespoons chopped fresh cilantro

To make the pita chips:
Preheat the oven to 450°F.

Split the pitas along the seam so each pita makes two circles. Brush oil on both sides of each circle and sprinkle lightly with Vege-Sal. Cut each circle in half, then cut each half into four triangles. (Each pita will yield 16 wedges.)

Divide the pita wedges between two baking sheets, arranging them in a single layer. Bake, one sheet at a time, until the chips are toasted and firm, but not completely crisp, about 5 minutes. Let the pita chips cool completely.

To make the guacamole:
Cut the avocados in half and remove the pits. Scoop the avocado meat into a medium bowl, mashing it with a spoon or potato masher to break up the chunks.

Add the cheese, onion, garlic, and lime juice and mix until nearly smooth, adding a few pinches each of salt and pepper to season the guacamole as you go along. Don't be shy—you will need at least 1 teaspoon of each to coax out the avocado flavor.

Garnish the guacamole with the cilantro and serve immediately with the pita chips.

This DIY version of chips and guacamole is sure to please. I've amped up the guacamole by adding tangy Havarti. Since Havarti is on the creamier side, be sure it's cold before you grate it or else you'll have a mess on your hands. Using pitas instead of tortillas for chips adds a unique flavor and crunch to this easy appetizer. Use your favorite seasoning but I love spike VegerSal Magic!

Red Pepper Hummus

⤳ Makes about 1½ cups

1 (13.5-ounce) can chickpeas, drained, 2 tablespoons of liquid reserved

¼ cup tahini paste, stirred well before measuring

¼ cup roasted red peppers, drained (I use Mezzetta brand)

2 tablespoons freshly squeezed lemon juice, or more to taste

2 teaspoons chili oil or 1 or 2 pinches dried chile flakes

3 garlic cloves, coarsely chopped

1 teaspoon kosher salt, or more to taste

Freshly ground black pepper

¼ cup extra-virgin olive oil

Flaky sea salt, such as Maldon (optional)

Pita chips (see page 91), carrot sticks, and radish slices, for serving

In a blender or food processor, combine the chickpeas and liquid, tahini, red peppers, lemon juice, chili oil, garlic, salt, and a generous pinch of pepper. Blend until smooth, scraping down the sides as needed. Taste, seasoning with more salt and lemon juice if desired. With the blender or processor running, drizzle in the olive oil.

Transfer to a serving bowl and garnish with a drizzle of olive oil, a squeeze of lemon juice, and a pinch of Maldon sea salt (if using). (At this point the hummus can be covered and stored in the refrigerator for up to 2 days before serving.) Serve with pita chips, carrots, radishes, and/or other fresh veggies of your choice.

A basic go-to hummus recipe always comes in handy, but I like it even better with roasted red peppers—that's one of the reasons I like to keep a jar on hand. Make the pita chips on page 91 for the ultimate accompaniment for this dip.

good for you

Kale Chips

Serves 2 to 4

1 bunch lacinato kale

1 tablespoon extra-virgin
olive oil

¼ teaspoon garlic salt,
such as Lawry's

Preheat the oven to 350°F and set the oven racks to the upper third and lower third of the oven. Line two rimmed baking sheets with aluminum foil.

Tear the leaves from the kale, discarding the tough stems. Tear the leaves into large pieces. In a large bowl, mix the kale, oil, and garlic salt. (I love to get in there with my hands and massage the kale to make sure it all gets evenly coated with the oil.) Divide the kale between the two baking sheets.

Bake the kale chips until crispy but not burned, 16 to 18 minutes, rotating the baking sheets between the two racks and 180 degrees halfway through cooking. For the best crunch factor, serve immediately.

When you're looking to balance out the carbo-load that tends to come with watching a game (or snacking in general), it's nice to surprise people with some crispy kale chips. Baking them makes them taste as if they were pulled out of a fryer...but the bonus is they're actually good for you.

The Cheese Plate

❦ Serves 10-ish

❧ The key to any game-worthy cheese plate is variety. My go-to cheese choices are Havarti with dill and Brie or another soft cheese. I also usually have a sharp white Cheddar. For a medium-bodied cheese, I like Tomme or Gruyère. To eat with the cheeses, I offer fig jam, toasted almonds, and black and green olives. Charcuterie of some sort—whether it's slices of prosciutto, capicola, or salami—makes the cheese plate more substantial. Salami goes great with Cheddar, so sometimes I put a whole salami on the platter that people can slice as they go. And you can't forget crackers—just choose your favorites. Finally, when they are in season, I always add grapes, though they have to be green grapes in my book. They're more refreshing.

Let's talk about one of the easiest—and best—ways to get food on the table on game day: Make a cheese plate. This is less of a recipe and more of a choose-your-own-adventure.

Island Ahi Tuna

⋆ Serves 4

1 pound sushi-grade
ahi tuna steaks, cut into
¼-inch cubes

½ cup mango cubes
(no bigger than ¼ inch)

¼ cup minced red onion

1 jalapeño, seeded
and minced

2 tablespoons freshly
squeezed lime juice

2 tablespoons
grapeseed oil

1 tablespoon rice vinegar

½ to 1 teaspoon chili oil
or 1 or 2 pinches dried
chile flakes

½ teaspoon dark
brown sugar

1 teaspoon flaky sea salt,
such as Maldon

Tortilla chips, for serving

In a large bowl, combine the tuna, mango, onion, and jalapeño.

In a small bowl, whisk together the lime juice, grapeseed oil, rice vinegar, chili oil, and brown sugar. Season with the salt.

Pour the seasoning sauce over the fish and mix well. Refrigerate for at least 5 minutes but no longer than 15 minutes to allow the flavors to meld. Serve immediately with tortilla chips.

Sometimes you want a little something special for game day. And what could be better than spiced-up ahi tuna scooped up with chips? Because I can't help myself, I add a pinch of dark brown sugar to draw out the sweetness of the mango. For best results, cut the mango into pieces no larger than the ahi.

Game Day Pasta

ᕒ Serves 4 to 6

2 tablespoons extra-virgin olive oil

½ cup finely diced yellow onion

Kosher salt

Freshly ground black pepper

4 garlic cloves, minced

1 globe eggplant, cut into cubes (about 6 cups)

1½ cups dry red wine

2 bay leaves

2 teaspoons tomato paste

1 (13.5-ounce) can whole San Marzano tomatoes, crushed with a spoon or your hands, including liquid

Pinch of dried thyme

2 teaspoons dark brown sugar

1 pound spaghetti or penne

2 packed cups spinach leaves

Handful of fresh basil leaves, chopped

1 or 2 lemon wedges

ᕒ Heat the oil in a large skillet or Dutch oven over medium heat. Add the onion, season with salt and pepper, and cook until softened, about 3 minutes. Add the garlic and cook for 1 more minute.

Add the eggplant and season with salt and pepper. Cook, stirring often, until the eggplant begins to soften, about 3 minutes. Add the wine and bay leaves, increase the heat to medium-high, and cook until the wine has reduced by half, about 5 minutes.

Stir in the tomato paste and cook for 30 seconds. Pour in the tomatoes and season with the thyme, brown sugar, and 1 teaspoon kosher salt. Cook, simmering gently over medium-low heat, until the tomatoes have thickened enough to lightly coat the back of a spoon, about

5 minutes. Be sure to crush the tomatoes with a wooden spoon if any large chunks remain. Fish out the bay leaves.

Meanwhile, bring a large pot of salted water to a boil. Add the pasta and cook according to the package directions.

Drain the pasta, reserving ½ cup of the pasta water. Return the pasta to the pot. Pour in the sauce, spinach, and basil, and mix with tongs to coat evenly. Squeeze lemon juice over the top and taste, seasoning with more salt if desired. If the pasta seems dry, drizzle in a splash of the reserved pasta cooking water.

To serve, mound the pasta on plates.

We're big on ritual in the Curry family. This pasta has become our official pregame fuel, for a good reason: Stephen needs to load up on carbs before doing all that running on the court. And since consistency is key when it comes to performing well, maybe my pasta has something to do with it. I always start with the same base—eggplant—and then sneak as many vegetables as I can into the pot. While pregame meals mean no cheese for Stephen (too much dairy is not good on the stomach), you can feel free to add a sprinkling of Parmesan on top if you'd like. I also often make the sauce to spoon over fish.

Maria's Andouille Sausage Egg Rolls

Serves 10 to 12

1 pound boneless, skinless chicken breasts, cut into ¼-inch pieces

Kosher salt

Freshly ground black pepper

Canola oil

8 ounces andouille sausage, cut into ¼-inch cubes

1 small red onion, finely diced

2 tablespoons pure maple syrup

2 tablespoons sweet chili sauce, such as Thai Kitchen or Mae Ploy, plus extra for dipping

8 ounces Cheddar cheese, cut into ¼-inch or smaller pieces, chilled

25 (6- to 8-inch) square egg roll wrappers

4 green onions (green parts only), thinly sliced

Season the chicken cubes with salt and pepper. Heat 1 tablespoon oil in a large nonstick skillet over medium-high heat. Sauté the chicken until cooked through and slightly golden brown, about 5 minutes. Transfer to a plate and let cool to room temperature.

Meanwhile, heat another 1 tablespoon oil in the same skillet over medium heat. Cook the sausage until brown, about 5 minutes. Add the red onion, maple syrup, and chili sauce and sauté until the liquid has thickened and clings to the sausage, 2 to 3 more minutes. (The mixture should not be saucy, because excess liquid and deep-frying are not a good combination.) Transfer the sausage mixture to a large bowl and let cool to room temperature.

When the sausage is cool, add the cheese and chicken and toss until well combined.

Set up a cutting board for filling and rolling the egg rolls. Next to it, place a small bowl of water for wetting the edges of the wrappers. Get out a platter for the ready-to-be-fried eggrolls.

To shape each egg roll, place the wrapper on the cutting board in a diamond shape. Spoon nearly ¼ cup of filling about 2 inches up from the bottom corner of the diamond. Lift the bottom corner up to cover the filling, then tuck the wrapper slightly under the filling and roll tightly halfway up.

Fold the two side corners toward the center, then continue to roll tightly until about 2 inches away from the top corner. Dampen that corner with a little water, then finish rolling, pressing firmly to seal it up. Transfer the finished egg roll to the platter. Repeat with the remaining wrappers until all the filling is used up.

(You may not need all the wrappers.)

In a 4-quart saucepan or Dutch oven, heat 2 inches of oil (5 to 6 cups oil, depending on the pan). Line a rimmed baking sheet with paper towels and have a slotted spoon or tongs handy. To test if the oil is hot enough, put the end of a wooden spoon in the oil and see if bubbles form around it. (The ideal oil temperature is 350°F; feel free to check it with a deep-fry thermometer.)

Working in batches to avoid crowding the pan, fry the egg rolls until deeply golden brown, about 2 to 3 minutes. Drain on paper towels. Serve while still hot, with a sprinkle of green onions on top and a little sweet chili sauce on the side for dipping.

If I could request only one thing for my sister Maria to make for me, it would have to be these egg rolls. Crunchy, salty, and slightly sweet, they are the perfect appetizers for nearly any event. The only problem is that there's never enough, no matter how many she makes. Thanks, Sis!

A few notes before you start: Cube all the ingredients about the same size so your egg rolls have a uniform bite. I start by cubing the cheese and then placing the cubes on a baking sheet in the freezer while I prepare the chicken and sausage. Make sure the chicken and sausage have cooled before you roll them in the wrappers. Look for egg roll wrappers in the refrigerated or frozen section of Asian grocery stores or well-stocked general grocery stores.

Sticky Honey-Garlic Baby Back Ribs

Serves 6

1 (2½- to 3-pound) rack baby back ribs

1 tablespoon garlic powder

1 tablespoon kosher salt

1½ teaspoons freshly ground black pepper

1½ packed cups dark brown sugar

1 cup water

½ cup honey

¼ cup minced yellow onion

8 garlic cloves, minced

Flaky sea salt, such as Maldon (optional)

Preheat the oven to 325°F. Line a heavy-duty roasting pan or rimmed baking sheet with aluminum foil (bottom and sides) and lightly oil it.

Put the rack of ribs in the prepared pan and season all over with the garlic powder, salt, and pepper. Bake for 30 minutes.

Increase the oven temperature to 450°F. Turn the ribs meaty-side down. Whisk together the sugar, water, honey, onion, and garlic. Pour the sauce over the ribs, cover tightly with foil, and bake until tender when pierced with a fork, about 1 hour. Uncover, turn the ribs meaty-side up, and bake until the ribs have crisped up, about 5 more minutes.

Transfer the rack to a large cutting board. When cool enough to handle, cut the ribs along the bones. Stack up the ribs on a plate, sprinkle with sea salt if desired, and serve.

I've been a sucker for sweet, sticky ribs ever since I started eating them at Kevin Garden, a favorite Chinese restaurant in Toronto. This recipe is a sweeter, more Southern take on ribs. Be sure to serve them with plenty of napkins. Also be sure to line the roasting pan thoroughly with aluminum foil—even up the sides—or else you're talking about a pan that will need to soak for a while before scrubbing.

You can also make the ribs the night before. Let the racks cool, then wrap them tightly and refrigerate overnight. The next day, gently warm in the oven before carving up.

Game Day Chili

❧ Serves 8 to 10 (and then some...)

2 tablespoons extra-virgin olive oil

1 pound lean ground lamb

1 pound mild Italian sausage, casings removed

1 red onion, diced

1 shallot, minced

4 garlic cloves, minced

2 red bell peppers, seeded and diced

2 yellow bell peppers, seeded and diced

1 jalapeño, seeded (if desired, for less heat) and diced

Kosher salt

1 (4-ounce) can tomato paste

¼ cup chili powder

1 tablespoon ground cumin

1 tablespoon dried oregano

1 teaspoon ground cinnamon

1 teaspoon dried chile flakes

1 (12-ounce) bottle beer (I like Stella Artois)

1 (28-ounce) can crushed San Marzano tomatoes or whole tomatoes crushed with a spoon or your hands, including liquid

1 (14-ounce) can crushed San Marzano tomatoes or whole tomatoes crushed with a spoon or your hands, including liquid

1 (15-ounce) can black beans, rinsed and drained

1 (15-ounce) can kidney beans, rinsed and drained

1 (15-ounce) can pinto beans, rinsed and drained

½ cup pure maple syrup

Cast-Iron Cornbread (page 108), for serving

Pickled peppers and onions, for serving

Sour cream, for serving

Grated Cheddar and/or Monterey Jack cheese, for serving

❧ Heat the oil in a large stockpot over medium-high heat. Add the lamb and sausage and cook, breaking up the meat into large pieces with a spoon, until the meat has begun to brown and caramelize, 5 to 7 minutes. Using a slotted spoon, transfer the meat to a bowl. Discard all but 2 tablespoons of the fat.

Add the onion, shallot, garlic, bell peppers, and jalapeño to the pot and cook until the onion begins to soften, about 6 minutes. Season with a few pinches of salt.

Return the meat to the pot and stir in the tomato paste, chili powder, cumin, oregano, cinnamon, chile flakes, and a few pinches of salt. Sauté for 2 to 3 more minutes. Pour in the beer to deglaze the pot, using a wooden spoon to dislodge any brown bits from the bottom of the pot, and bring to a boil.

Pour in the tomatoes, beans, and maple syrup. Stir to combine all the ingredients and bring to a simmer. Lower the heat to medium-low and simmer until all the flavors have melded and the beans and tomatoes have thickened up to your preferred consistency for chili, about 1 hour.

Serve with the delicious cornbread, and offer pickled peppers and onions, sour cream, and grated cheese for toppings.

Canned tomatoes and beans, some ground meat, and a few dried herbs and spices—it's amazing that such deliciousness can come from these humble beginnings. The hardest part of this recipe is getting all the ingredients organized and prepped for the chili. Then the recipe takes care of itself. I give a nod to Canada in this recipe with a good glug of maple syrup. It's not enough to make this sweet, but it does round out the flavors of the spices. For the win, serve this chili with my rich Cast-Iron Cornbread (page 108).

Cast-Iron Cornbread

૪ Serves 8 to 10

1¼ cups cornmeal

¾ cup all-purpose flour

¼ packed cup dark brown
sugar, plus 2 tablespoons
for sprinkling on top

2 teaspoons baking
powder

½ teaspoon baking soda

1 teaspoon kosher salt

¾ cup whole milk

1 (14¾-ounce) can sweet
creamed corn

1 (8-ounce) container
mascarpone cheese

2 large eggs, lightly beaten

8 tablespoons (1 stick)
unsalted butter, melted

◦૪◦ Preheat the oven
to 450°F. Oil a 12-inch,
well-seasoned cast-iron
skillet.

In a large bowl, whisk
together the cornmeal,
flour, ¼ cup brown sugar,
baking powder, baking
soda, and salt.

In a smaller bowl, whisk
together the milk, creamed
corn, mascarpone, and eggs.
Gently stir the wet mixture
into the dry ingredients until
well combined, then stir in
the melted butter.

Pour the batter into the
skillet and sprinkle with the
remaining 2 tablespoons
brown sugar. Bake until the
top is golden brown and a
toothpick inserted into the
center comes out clean,
about 25 minutes. Let cool
for at least 5 minutes before
cutting into wedges and
serving.

Game Day Chili (page 106) just wouldn't be the same without a side of cornbread. Laced with mascarpone cheese
and creamed corn, this recipe makes a decadent, dense, and
extremely moist cornbread. I bake it directly in a cast-iron
skillet for an addictive crust.

Making Dinner Happen

DINNER AT OUR HOME is definitely a big deal. I just *love* preparing a satisfying meal for my family. Cooking is my creative outlet, and dinner is the meal that allows my passion and imagination to run wild. I love trying unfamiliar ingredients, exploring new recipe ideas, and tweaking family favorites, and the late afternoon and early evening is the best time of the day to do so. By that time, (most of) the craziness of the day is over and the environment in our house is much more relaxed and playful.

I should add that we are all a bunch of goofballs around here. Growing up, both Stephen and I were the main sources of silliness in our families. For me, that meant that at dinnertime—like clockwork—I would drop to the floor and start rolling around, saying, "I'm a steamroller!" This went on throughout high school, and I have no idea why. I'll let Stephen tell his own goofy stories, but let's just say he's planted fake snakes at golf courses before...! Needless to say, we still hold on to our super silly ways, and our little ones are quickly picking up the family tradition. Dinner is the perfect time to let loose and laugh—a lot.

Dinner is also the meal that draws in the most memories. When Stephen was drafted, on June 25, 2009, it was a long, long night. We never slept, and then just got on a plane and flew to San Francisco. The Warriors took us out to a beautiful restaurant in the city called

Crustacean, which is where we learned to love Dungeness crab. It was a monumental moment, a start of a new chapter in everyone's life.

All the recipes in this chapter are inspired by something or someone special. Some, like Mama Alexander's Brown Sugar Chicken (page 132) are hands down inspired by my mom. The Jamaican-style escovitch recipe (page 113) is from my beautiful grandma. Others are inspired by a special restaurant meal, a new ingredient, or a moment in time. I hope you enjoy them as much as we do.

Here's to happy bellies and smiling faces!

MAIN COURSES

Gwendolyn's Escovitch

Serves 4

SAUCE

1 red bell pepper, seeded and thinly sliced

1 yellow or orange bell pepper, seeded and thinly sliced

2 Scotch bonnet peppers, left whole (or 1 serrano for milder heat)

1 large yellow onion, sliced

1 large carrot, peeled and cut into matchsticks

1 cup distilled white vinegar

6 allspice berries

1 to 2 tablespoons sugar

Pinch of kosher salt

¼ teaspoon freshly ground black pepper

FISH

¼ cup all-purpose flour

½ teaspoon paprika

½ teaspoon garlic powder

Kosher salt

Freshly ground black pepper

4 (4- to 6-ounce) red snapper fillets

½ cup canola oil

To make the sauce: In a large skillet, combine all the sauce ingredients (start with 1 tablespoon sugar) and bring to a simmer over medium heat. Cook until the peppers soften and the vinegar is infused with the chiles and allspice, about 5 minutes. Taste, adding up to another 1 tablespoon sugar if it's too sour for your liking. Remove the Scotch bonnets if heat isn't for you. Or, if you like it spicy, cut one in half and put it back in.

continued on page 114

My grandma, Gwendolyn, is a gorgeous six-foot-tall Jamaican woman. She has been living in Canada (where I was born) for decades and still has her beautiful accent. And she still makes all my favorite Jamaican meals—jerk pork and curry goat are a couple of her specialties. My number-one pick, however, is her escovitch, a fish dish made with a sweet-and-sour sauce, almost like pickling liquid. Its vibrant flavors and presentation are a perfect representation of her personality.

The sauce for this dish can be made well in advance and stored in the refrigerator. Simply reheat it in a skillet or saucepan when you are ready to cook the fish. For a lighter (but just as delicious) take on classic Jamaican escovitch, use a whole snapper instead of fillets. Stuff lemon and thyme inside the fish and cook it on the grill. Be sure to coat the fish with oil so that the skin does not stick to the grill grates. Either way, serve the escovitch with icy-cold ginger beer for the full effect.

To make the fish: Put the flour on a plate and season with the paprika, garlic powder, and a generous pinch each of salt and pepper. Dredge the fish in the seasoned flour to give it a light, even coating and pat off any excess.

Line a plate with paper towels. Heat a large cast-iron skillet over medium-high heat and add the oil. When the oil is hot, pan-fry the fish until golden brown on both sides, about 2 minutes per side. Using a spatula, transfer the fillets to the paper towel–lined plate.

Transfer the fish to a platter and pour the sauce on top. Serve immediately so the fish doesn't get too soft.

Apricot-Glazed Salmon with Summer Squash and Zucchini

Serves 2 grown-ups (and 1 child)

2 zucchini, diced

1 yellow summer squash, diced

1 cup supersweet corn kernels (from about 1 cob)

1 tablespoon extra-virgin olive oil

Kosher salt

Freshly ground black pepper

¼ cup low-sodium soy sauce

2 heaping tablespoons apricot preserves

3 garlic cloves, minced

1 (8- to 12-ounce) salmon fillet

Preheat the oven to 425°F. Have a large Dutch oven or roasting pan handy.

Put the zucchini, summer squash, and corn in the Dutch oven and coat with the olive oil and a pinch each of salt and pepper.

In a small bowl, stir together the soy sauce, apricot preserves, and garlic.

Place the salmon fillet in the Dutch oven, nestling it into the veggies. Pour the apricot sauce over the top. Bake until the veggies are cooked and the salmon flakes easily when pierced with a fork, about 15 minutes.

To serve, divide the salmon between 2 plates and spoon the vegetables alongside.

This is my go-to recipe for salmon. It's one of those recipes that's easy to pull together, especially in the summer when zucchini and corn are everywhere, but it always surpasses expectations. The secret ingredients for deliciousness: apricot preserves and soy sauce, which give the salmon a beautiful, salty-sweet glaze. Before you start, make sure you have a Dutch oven or roasting pan that will comfortably fit the salmon and vegetables.

Soy-Citrus Salmon

Juice of 1 orange
(about ⅓ cup)

Juice of 1 lime (about
3 tablespoons)

¼ cup low-sodium
soy sauce

¼ cup mirin

2 tablespoons honey

2 tablespoons dark
brown sugar

4 garlic cloves, minced

4 green onions,
thinly sliced

4 (4- to 6-ounce)
salmon fillets

Kosher salt

Freshly ground black pepper

Preheat the oven to 425°F. Oil a 9-by-13-inch baking dish.

To make the sauce, whisk together the orange and lime juice, soy sauce, mirin, honey, brown sugar, garlic, and green onions. Voilà—your sauce is done.

Put the salmon in the baking dish. Season with salt and pepper. Pour the sauce over the fish, piling the green onion and garlic pieces on top. Bake until the salmon flakes easily when pierced with a fork, about 10 minutes.

To serve, spoon the sauce in the pan over each salmon fillet and over any roasted vegetables served alongside.

I am always on the hunt for new ways to make meals that are quick and easy but not lacking in flavor. This was one of those slam-dunk successes, getting the job done in both the flavor and time departments. The sauce can be used as a marinade for other fish or poultry. (Chicken can be marinated overnight.) To round out the meal, serve the salmon with Herb-Roasted Potatoes with Lime (page 171) and grilled or roasted asparagus (see the instructions for cooking the asparagus in the recipe for Grilled Spiced Chicken and Asparagus with Parsley-Mint Sauce on page 134).

Sweet and Savory Shrimp and Grits

⁂ Serves 4

⁂ GRITS ⁂

1 cup grits (preferably quick-cooking)

½ cup shredded mild Cheddar cheese

½ cup shredded fontina cheese

2 tablespoons unsalted butter

1 teaspoon truffle oil (optional)

Kosher salt

Freshly ground black pepper

⁂ SHRIMP ⁂

3 slices thick-cut bacon

½ cup minced yellow onion

1 yellow bell pepper, seeded and diced

1 orange or red bell pepper, seeded and diced

Kosher salt

Freshly ground black pepper

3 garlic cloves, minced

1½ pounds extra jumbo shrimp (16 to 20 per pound), peeled and deveined (see page 124)

2 tablespoons dark brown sugar

½ cup lighter-style white wine (I use Riesling)

2 tablespoons freshly squeezed lemon juice

Chopped fresh flat-leaf parsley, for garnish

Green onions, thinly sliced, for garnish

⁂ To make the grits: Cook the grits according to the directions on the package. Once the grits are cooked through, stir in the Cheddar and fontina cheeses, butter, truffle oil (if using), and salt and pepper to taste. Keep warm.

To make the shrimp: Line a plate with paper towels. In a heavy skillet over medium-low heat, fry the bacon until most of the fat has rendered and the bacon is crisp, about 10 minutes. Transfer the bacon to the paper towels and discard all but 3 tablespoons of the fat in the skillet. Chop up the bacon and set aside.

When made right, shrimp and grits are an unbeatable duo. This recipe is a complete meal on its own, requiring no salads or sides. For my take, I give the shrimp a bit of sweetness with dark brown sugar (one of my favorite ingredients, as you might have noticed). This makes the shrimp both sweet and savory.

For grits, save yourself extra effort and buy quick-cooking grits. Quaker makes a dependable one. If using slow-cooked grits, that's fine, too. Just follow the cooking instructions on the package and allow for more time (and patience).

In the remaining fat in the skillet, sauté the onion over medium heat until it begins to soften (but before it starts to brown), about 3 minutes. Add the bell peppers and season with a pinch each of salt and pepper. Cook until the peppers have softened, about 3 minutes. Add the garlic and cook until fragrant, about 1 minute longer. Push the mixture to one side of the pan.

Add the shrimp to the empty side of the pan and cook until they begin to turn pink, about 2 minutes. Sprinkle the brown sugar evenly over the shrimp and cook, stirring, for 30 seconds more.

Increase the heat to medium-high. Pour in the wine and cook, scraping any caramelized bits off the bottom of the pan with a wooden spoon. Reduce the wine by half, 2 to 3 minutes. Stir in the lemon juice and season with salt and pepper to taste.

To serve, pour the grits into a large warmed serving bowl. Pour the shrimp and any sauce over the grits. Sprinkle the reserved bacon, parsley, and green onion over the top to finish. Serve hot.

Honey-Pepper Shrimp

❧ Serves 6

❧ HONEY-PEPPER SAUCE ❧

2 tablespoons canola oil

½ cup minced
yellow onion

2 teaspoons minced garlic

2 tablespoons minced
fresh ginger

½ cup rice wine vinegar

½ cup honey

2 teaspoons fish sauce

1½ teaspoons crushed
pink peppercorns
(optional)

1 teaspoon freshly ground
black pepper, or more
if desired

❧ SHRIMP ❧

Canola oil, for frying

2 pounds jumbo shrimp (21
to 25 per pound), peeled
and deveined

1 teaspoon kosher salt

1 tablespoon
all-purpose flour

4 cups Steamed Jasmine
Rice (page 168) or several
large lettuce leaves, for
serving

To make the sauce:
Heat the oil in a small skillet over medium heat. Sauté the onion, garlic, and ginger until the onion is translucent, about 3 minutes. (If the garlic starts to turn golden brown, lower the heat.) Add the vinegar, honey, fish sauce, pink peppercorns (if using), and black pepper. Increase the heat to medium-high and simmer until the sauce is thick enough to coat the back of a spoon, about 6 minutes. Keep the sauce warm while you make the shrimp.

To make the shrimp: In a 4-quart saucepan or Dutch oven, heat 1 inch of oil (about 3 cups oil, depending on the pan). Line a plate with paper towels and have a slotted spoon handy. To test if the oil is hot enough, put the end of a wooden spoon in the oil and see if bubbles form around it. (The ideal oil temperature is 350°F; feel free to check it with a deep-fry thermometer.)

Put the shrimp in a bowl and season with the salt. Sprinkle with the flour and toss to coat the shrimp evenly. Working in batches to avoid crowding the pan, fry the shrimp, using a slotted spoon to keep them from sticking together, until pink and opaque and lightly crisp, 1 to 2 minutes. Using the slotted spoon, transfer the shrimp to the paper towel–lined plate to drain off excess oil. Repeat with the remaining shrimp.

To serve, put the shrimp in a bowl, pour the sauce over the top and toss gently to coat. Serve hot over rice or in lettuce cups.

The first time I tried pink peppercorns, it was in a dessert of all places—an apple cake in which the peppercorns dotted the whipped cream. The delicate, almost floral peppercorns worked surprisingly well with the sweet cake, and I've had a soft spot for them ever since. With honey in the sauce, this shrimp dish is on the sweeter side, so my mind went back to those peppercorns to counter some of the sweetness. The sauce has a good amount of black pepper, too, so all is not lost if pink peppercorns are out of reach. But if you can find them, do include them—it's so very worth it.

How to Peel and Devein Shrimp

While you can buy shrimp already peeled, if you're buying frozen shrimp (and many good-quality Gulf shrimp are sold this way), you're probably going to have to peel them. Fortunately, it's easy to do and pretty forgiving. To peel the shrimp, turn the shrimp over so its belly faces up and peel back the shell toward its back. This will crack the shell, loosening it and making it easy to pull off. To pull off the tail, hold it and pull, twisting it a bit to loosen. Next, you can devein the shrimp—which means removing the gritty digestive track that runs from the head to the tail. To do so, use a paring knife to cut along the back of the shrimp and expose the vein. Using the tip of the knife or a bamboo skewer, pull the vein up to remove it.

Salt-Baked Branzino

⅋ Serves 4

4 large egg whites

4 cups kosher salt

2 teaspoons fennel seed

2 whole branzino
(12 ounces to 1 pound
each), gutted and scaled

2 lemons, 1 thinly sliced
and 1 cut into wedges,
for serving

A handful each of sage
sprigs, rosemary sprigs,
and thyme sprigs

Extra-virgin olive oil,
for garnish (optional)

Freshly ground black
pepper, for garnish
(optional)

Preheat the oven to 450°F. Line a large roasting pan or rimmed baking sheet with parchment paper and have a warm serving platter ready. Take the fish out of the refrigerator at least 15 minutes before cooking.

In a bowl, whisk together the egg whites and salt. It should look like wet sand. (This will be the paste you'll use to coat the fish.)

In a small sauté pan, toast the fennel over medium heat until fragrant, about 30 seconds.

With paper towels, pat the fish dry inside and out. Fill each fish with 1 teaspoon fennel seeds, half of the sliced lemon, and half of the herbs.

Line the bottom of the pan with a layer of the salt paste about ¼ inch thick. Nestle the fish onto the layer of salt, leaving a couple of inches between the two fish, and cover with the rest of the salt paste, using your hands to pat the salt over each fish to ensure it is completely covered.

continued on page 126

Joso's restaurant in Toronto is a favorite in my family because of its seafood. They serve beautiful whole roasted fish tableside, removing the bones and serving the fillets right in front of you. The whole experience is part of the reason I have always loved a nice, roasted whole fish. When I became confident enough in the kitchen, I knew I had to try it for myself.

When you bake fish, it can easily turn dry or lack flavor. I found a way around this is by using a chef trick: encasing the fish in an "igloo" of salt. Sounds intimidating, I know, but it is easy. Putting a salt crust on the outside skin of the fish ensures that the meat will be tender and perfectly salted inside. It's also a visual crowd pleaser, so if you're entertaining guests and want a party trick, this is the way to go. You can even use a hammer to crack the shell at the table to unveil the whole fish...although I admit that this is overkill. (Tapping it with a spoon works just as well.)

Salt-Baked Branzino, continued

Bake the fish, rotating the pan once, for 30 minutes. The salt will have turned a deep golden color and should feel as hard as a rock if tapped. Remove the pan from the oven and let it rest for 10 minutes.

Tap the salt "igloo" with a spoon or the back of a knife (or even that hammer!) to break the shell, then carefully remove the pieces. The fish under the salt shell will be moist and flaky.

To serve the fish, peel back the top layer of skin and use a metal fish spatula or long offset spatula to carefully remove the top fillet. Place on the warm serving platter. Lift up the tail and pull it toward the head. The tail and most of the fish skeleton should come with it. Discard the skeleton, along with the herbs and lemon slices, and then remove the bottom fillet and place on the platter. Repeat with the remaining fish. Drizzle the fish with olive oil and sprinkle with a little pepper—or eat it as is, which is what I do. Serve with lemon wedges alongside.

Quick Tip

Branzino, a type of sea bass, is mild and easy to like. Because it's farmed, it's also becoming easier to find in grocery stores. If you can't find whole branzino, trout is a good substitute. You can even use this salt-baking method with snapper, although a whole snapper tends to be a little bigger than branzino or trout. Before taking the fish home, ask the fishmonger to scale it for you—they don't necessarily do this unless you ask.

Seafood Medley

⁓ Serves 6

1 pound large dry-packed scallops (8 to 12 scallops), side muscles removed

Kosher salt

Freshly ground black pepper

1 tablespoon extra-virgin olive oil

4 tablespoons (½ stick) unsalted butter

2 garlic cloves, minced

1 teaspoon ground turmeric

1 cup dry white wine, such as Sauvignon Blanc

1 (28-ounce) can San Marzano tomatoes, chopped, including liquid

Juice of ½ lemon (about 2 tablespoons)

1 tablespoon sugar

1 pound mussels, debearded (see sidebar)

1 pound jumbo shrimp (21 to 25 per pound), peeled (preferably with the tails left on) and deveined (see page 124)

½ cup chopped fresh flat-leaf parsley

1 lemon, cut into wedges

Sourdough or other crusty bread, for serving

Pat the scallops dry with a paper towel and season with salt and pepper.

Heat the oil in a large Dutch oven or heavy-bottomed pot over medium-high heat. Sear the scallops on one side until deep golden brown, about 4 minutes (for the best sear, avoid the temptation to move the scallops around). Flip the scallops and sear the other side briefly—the scallops will be cooked further in the sauce, so it's best to slightly under-cook them at this point. Remove the scallops from the pan and keep warm.

In the same Dutch oven, lower the heat to medium and melt the butter. Add the garlic and cook until aromatic and golden, about 1 minute. Add the turmeric and pour in the wine. Cook until reduced by half, about 3 minutes. Pour in the tomatoes and lemon juice and season with the sugar and a pinch each of salt and pepper. Raise the heat to medium-high and simmer briskly until the tomatoes have thickened into a sauce, about 7 minutes.

continued on page 130 ⤳

As I said about my Carolina Chowder recipe (page 76), crustaceans are my jam. But really, I love all seafood in general. A hearty bowl of steamed mussels or a plate of seared scallops can make a meal on their own, but put them together with shrimp, garlic, white wine, and turmeric and we're talking a whole new experience. Serve with a hearty, crusty bread to sop up the juices.

If you've never worked with mussels, don't freak out. It's actually pretty easy—see the sidebar. And for information on buying and preparing scallops, check out the recipe for Sweet Pea Soup with Herbed Scallops (page 67).

Seafood Medley, continued

Add the mussels and shrimp and season with another pinch of salt and pepper. Lower the heat to medium, cover the Dutch oven, and cook until the mussels have opened and the shrimp are pink, about 5 minutes. (Discard any mussels that failed to open.) Return the scallops to the Dutch oven and simmer for another minute or so to warm them through.

Sprinkle the parsley over the stew right before serving. Serve with lemon wedges and bread.

How to Prepare Mussels

Since you buy mussels live, plan on cooking them the day you buy them—just put them in the refrigerator in a bowl covered with a damp towel until you're ready to cook them. Pick through the mussels to ensure that all of them are closed, and discard any with broken shells. If you find a mussel that is gaping open, pinch the shell closed and see if it stays that way. If it reopens, toss it out to be safe. Right before cooking, use your fingers or a pair of pliers to pull off the "beard" of the mussel, which is the hairy thing near the base of the shell, if you see it. And that's all you have to do!

Mama Alexander's Brown Sugar Chicken

⅋ Serves 4

4 whole chicken legs, drumsticks and thighs attached (about 3½ pounds)

Kosher salt

Freshly ground black pepper

1 tablespoon unsalted butter

1 tablespoon extra-virgin olive oil

2 tablespoons minced shallot

3 garlic cloves, minced

¾ cup chicken broth

1 cup low-sodium soy sauce

2 packed cups dark brown sugar

1 heaping tablespoon minced fresh ginger

4 cups Steamed Jasmine Rice (page 168)

Preheat the oven to 350°F. Season the chicken with salt and pepper.

In a 5½-quart or larger Dutch oven or a heavy oven-safe saucepan, melt the butter with the olive oil over medium-high heat. Working in two batches, brown the chicken until golden brown, about 5 minutes per side. Transfer the chicken pieces to a plate.

Pour off all but 1 tablespoon of fat and return the Dutch oven to medium heat. Sauté the shallot until translucent, about 1 minute, adding the garlic halfway through cooking. Add the chicken broth and bring to a boil, dislodging any caramelized bits from the bottom of the Dutch oven to maximize flavor. (I'm hungry already!)

Stir in the soy sauce, brown sugar, and ginger. Simmer to dissolve the sugar and thicken the sauce slightly, 3 to 5 minutes. Put the chicken back into the Dutch oven, skin-side up, and cover with the lid. Bake for 30 minutes. Remove the lid and bake until the chicken is nearly falling off the bone, about 30 minutes more (test a piece by piercing with a fork to see if the meat pulls away easily).

To serve, put a chicken leg on each plate. Spoon some rice next to the chicken and drizzle some of the sauce over both. Mmm mmm mmm!

If you try only one recipe in this book, let it be this one. At least once a week my mom would make this "sweet chicken" as we called it, usually upon my request. It's a sticky, sweet, fall-off-the-bone chicken dish that (to me) is second to none—truly a sweet and savory combo at its finest. Even though I have two little girls of my own now, I still ask my mom to make it every time she comes to visit.

If you're looking for a vegetable to pair with it beyond the usual suspects, here's what my mom does: She cuts an acorn squash in half, scoops out the seeds (but leaves the skin on), and then slices it into planks. She sprinkles the squash planks with cinnamon, salt, and black pepper and then roasts it in the oven alongside the chicken.

Grilled Spiced Chicken and Asparagus with Parsley-Mint Sauce

⌀ Serves 4

2 tablespoons paprika

1 teaspoon
ground cinnamon

¼ teaspoon
ground cumin

Kosher salt

Freshly ground
black pepper

4 boneless, skinless
chicken breasts (about
1½ pounds total)

1 bunch asparagus (about
12 ounces), trimmed

Extra-virgin olive oil

4 cups Steamed Jasmine
Rice (page 168)

1 recipe Parsley-Mint
Sauce (page 162)

⌀ Preheat an outdoor grill or have a cast-iron grill pan handy. If using a grill pan for the chicken, preheat the oven to 400°F for the asparagus (which won't easily fit on a grill pan) and line a rimmed baking sheet with aluminum foil. If using a grill for the chicken, you'll use it for the asparagus, too.

In a small bowl, combine the paprika, cinnamon, cumin, 2 teaspoons salt, and ½ teaspoon pepper. Coat one piece of chicken at a time in the spice mixture, then transfer to a large plate.

Lightly coat the asparagus in olive oil and season with a pinch each of salt and pepper.

If using a grill pan, preheat the pan over medium-high heat.

Grill the chicken until cooked through and dark grill marks appear, 4 to 6 minutes per side. Let it rest while you cook the asparagus. If using a grill, place the asparagus perpendicular to the grill grates so they don't fall through (or use a grill basket) and grill until slightly charred and softened but still firm in the center, about 4 minutes depending on the thickness of the asparagus. If using the oven, roast the asparagus on the foil-lined baking sheet until brown at the tips and softened but still firm in the center, 6 to 8 minutes.

Serve each chicken breast with a side of asparagus and rice. Spoon some of the sauce over the chicken and asparagus and serve the rest at the table.

If you need an excuse to try out the Parsley-Mint Sauce on page 162 (not that you really need an excuse), here you go. This is the perfect dish to make when spring gets going and produce departments have stacks of beautiful asparagus. I've given instructions for both an outdoor grill and a stovetop grill pan, so use whatever you're most comfortable with.

Orange-Thyme Chicken Thighs with Carrot Puree

⅌ Serves 4 to 6

⅌ CHICKEN ⅌

8 bone-in, skin-on chicken thighs (about 3¾ pounds)

Salt and pepper, to taste

1 tablespoon extra-virgin olive oil

1 tablespoon unsalted butter

1 shallot, chopped

3 garlic cloves, chopped

½ cup dry white wine

½ cup orange juice

1 tablespoon honey

Leaves from 3 thyme sprigs

⅌ CARROTS ⅌

2 cups chopped carrots

Salt and pepper, to taste

¼ cup heavy cream, at room temperature

1 tablespoon unsalted butter, at room temperature

¼ teaspoon ground cumin

⅌ To make the chicken: Preheat the oven to 425°F. Season the chicken thighs generously on all sides with salt and pepper.

Heat the oil in a cast-iron skillet over medium-high heat. In two batches, brown the chicken thighs, skin-side down, until golden brown, 3 to 5 minutes for each batch. Transfer the chicken to a plate. Discard all but 1 tablespoon of the fat in the pan.

Lower the heat to medium and melt the butter. Sauté the shallot until translucent, about 1 minute, adding the garlic halfway through cooking. Add the wine and orange juice and bring to a boil, dislodging any bits of food from the bottom of the pan with a wooden spoon. Stir in the honey and thyme and simmer until the sauce has reduced slightly, 3 to 5 minutes.

Remove the pan from the heat and put the chicken back in the skillet, skin side up. Bake the thighs until tender when pierced with a fork, about 30 minutes. Let the chicken rest in their juices while you make the carrot puree.

To make the carrot puree: Put the carrots and a few pinches of salt in a saucepan and cover with water. Bring to a boil over high heat, then lower the heat to medium-low and simmer until the carrots just begin to turn tender, about 12 minutes. Drain the carrots and transfer to a blender. Add the cream, butter, and cumin and blend until smooth. Season with a few generous pinches each of salt and pepper.

To serve, spoon the carrot puree onto serving plates and top with the chicken thighs.

When I was making this recipe for the first time, I really wasn't sure how it would come out. Fortunately, it was a winner. It's hearty enough to serve for dinner guests, but light enough that it doesn't make you feel like taking a nap at the table. The flavors of the chicken and carrot are subtle, but the cumin and cream in the carrots and the orange juice in the sauce help liven things up. Plus, carrot puree is a great alternative to mashed potatoes any day. For serving sizes, small appetites will be satisfied with one chicken thigh, but count on two thighs each if everyone is really hungry.

Lemon-Beer Chicken

⅌ Serves 4 to 6

4 whole chicken legs,
drumsticks and
thighs attached
(about 3½ pounds)

Kosher salt

Freshly ground
black pepper

4 tablespoons (½ stick)
salted butter,
cut into cubes

2 lemons

½ cup lager-style beer

¼ cup sour cream

¼ cup minced shallot
(about 2)

3 garlic cloves, minced

1 teaspoon dried oregano

¼ teaspoon dried
chile flakes

2 tablespoons chopped
fresh flat-leaf parsley

Flaky sea salt, such as
Maldon, for garnish
(optional)

❧ Preheat the oven to 425°F. Season the chicken all over with salt and pepper. Scatter the butter cubes in a large baking dish and put the chicken pieces on top, skin-side up.

Zest the lemons and cut each lemon in half. Set aside the zest and one lemon half. Juice the remaining three lemon halves (you should have about 6 tablespoons juice).

Pour the lemon juice and beer into the dish and bake the chicken for 35 minutes.

While the chicken is baking, in a bowl whisk together the lemon zest, sour cream, shallot, garlic, oregano, chile flakes, and ¼ teaspoon each salt and pepper. After the chicken has baked for 35 minutes, spread the skin with the sour cream mixture and continue to bake until the skin is crispy and golden brown, an additional 30 minutes.

Transfer the chicken and any juices to a serving dish. Squeeze the remaining lemon half over the chicken. Sprinkle with the parsley and season with a pinch or two of Maldon salt for a little crunch, if desired. Serve hot.

Lemon juice, beer, and (yes!) butter flavor these chicken legs perfectly while keeping them juicy. To make the chicken skin even tastier, I spread a mixture of sour cream, lemon zest, shallot, garlic, and spices on top of the chicken halfway through the roasting process.

Jerk
TURKEY

Jerk Turkey

Serves 6, with extra for sandwiches

8 tablespoons (1 stick) salted butter, at room temperature

4 garlic cloves, coarsely chopped

2 green onions, coarsely chopped

1 shallot, coarsely chopped

Leaves from 3 thyme sprigs

½ teaspoon ground cloves

½ teaspoon ground allspice

½ teaspoon freshly ground black pepper

2 boneless, skin-on turkey breasts (about 1½ pounds each)

¾ cup low-sodium chicken or vegetable broth

¼ cup low-sodium soy sauce

1 recipe Spiced Butternut Squash Mash (page 174), for serving

Preheat the oven to 375°F.

In a food processor, pulse together the butter, garlic, green onions, shallot, thyme, cloves, allspice, and black pepper until a chunky compound butter forms, about 30 seconds.

Pat the turkey breasts with paper towels so the skin is completely dry. This will help the butter stick to the skin. Divide the butter in half and spread it over the skin of each turkey breast. It's okay if it doesn't look perfect—use your hands to press the butter onto the skin.

Place the turkey breasts, skin-side up, in a 9-by-13-inch baking dish and bake for 30 minutes. Combine the broth and soy sauce and pour into the baking dish. Continue to bake the turkey until the skin is golden brown and crispy and the breasts have cooked all the way though, about 30 more minutes. If using an instant-read meat thermometer, the internal temperature at the thickest part of the breast should be about 160°F. (The turkey will continue to cook after it's pulled out of the oven.)

Let the turkey rest for about 15 minutes to give the juices time to reabsorb into the meat. Slice one turkey breast into thick slices and serve on top of the butternut squash mash. Cool the other turkey breast to room temperature, then cover and refrigerate. Slice thinly and use for sandwiches or salads during the week.

I developed this recipe with my mom as a way to introduce people to Caribbean food in a kinder, gentler way (meaning no Scotch bonnet peppers to light your tongue on fire). I think we nailed it. When served with Spiced Butternut Squash Mash (page 174), it's the perfect mix of subtly spicy turkey and sweet, sweet squash. Instead of turkey breasts, feel free to substitute three or four chicken breasts—just cut the cook time a little bit.

Pork Chops and Apples

ॐ Serves 4

1 teaspoon chili powder

1 teaspoon kosher salt

½ teaspoon freshly ground black pepper

4 (1-inch-thick) bone-in pork chops

2 tablespoons extra-virgin olive oil

2 tablespoons unsalted butter

4 apples (preferably Pink Lady), cored and sliced

¼ teaspoon ground cinnamon

2 tablespoons pure maple syrup

Preheat the oven to 250°F. Put a rimmed baking sheet in the oven.

In a small bowl, combine the chili powder, salt, and pepper. Season the pork chops on both sides with the spice mix.

Heat the oil in a large non-stick skillet over medium-high heat. Sear the pork chops on both sides until golden brown on the outside and still a little pink in the center, about 3 minutes per side.

Turn off the oven and transfer the pork chops to the warmed baking sheet in the oven. Cook the remaining two chops and transfer them to the oven when finished.

In the same skillet, melt the butter. Add the apples and season with the cinnamon. Cook, stirring often, until the apples soften and caramelize around the edges, about 10 minutes, adding the syrup halfway through cooking.

To serve, transfer the apples to a platter and put the pork chops on top. Or, if the pan is big enough, add the chops back to the pan to coat in the sauce.

I always serve these pork chops with the Best Mac and Cheese (page 166). Always. It just makes sense to go all-out Southern with this one. I buy thin-cut pork chops because thick-cut ones require much more time to heat up near the bone. This lets me cook the apples in the same pan so they can caramelize beautifully in the pork juices. If bone-in chops are not available, use boneless chops—you might be able to shave a minute or so off the cooking time.

Olive and Mushroom–Smothered Pork Tenderloin

୫ Serves 8

୫ OLIVE-MUSHROOM SPREAD ୫

4 tablespoons extra-virgin olive oil

1 cup sliced cremini mushrooms

½ cup finely chopped yellow onion

6 garlic cloves, coarsely chopped

Kosher salt

Freshly ground black pepper

1 (6-ounce) can pitted black olives, drained

1 heaping tablespoon capers

୫ PORK ୫

1 teaspoon paprika

1 teaspoon dried thyme

1 teaspoon kosher salt

½ teaspoon freshly ground black pepper

2 pork tenderloins (about 2½ pounds total)

2 tablespoons extra-virgin olive oil

To make the olive-mushroom spread: In a large skillet, heat 1 tablespoon of the oil over medium-high heat. Cook the mushrooms until they begin to caramelize at the edges and have lost most of their water, about 3 minutes. Add the onion, lower the heat to medium, and cook until the onion begins to turn translucent, about 3 minutes. Add the garlic and cook for 1 more minute. Season with a pinch each of salt and pepper.

Transfer the mushroom mixture to a food processor, add the olives and capers, and pulse until coarsely chopped. You may have to pulse a few times to break up the olives. Taste, seasoning with a pinch of salt and pepper if desired (keep in mind that the olives are already quite salty). With the food processor running, drizzle in the remaining 3 tablespoons olive oil until a chunky paste forms. Set aside.

To make the pork: Preheat the oven to 450°F. Line a rimmed baking sheet with aluminum foil.

In a small bowl, combine the paprika, thyme, salt, and pepper. Rub the spices into the tenderloins.

Heat the oil in a skillet over medium-high heat. In batches, brown each side of the tenderloins until golden brown, 1 to 2 minutes per side. Place the tenderloins on the prepared baking sheet. Coat each tenderloin with a thick layer of the olive-mushroom spread and bake until cooked through, 20 to 25 minutes. If using an instant-read meat thermometer, the internal temperature at the thickest part of the tenderloin should reach 140°F. (It will continue to cook as it cools.)

Let the pork rest for at least 5 minutes or up to 15 minutes to give the juices time to reabsorb into the meat. Cut into thick slices to serve.

When I want to please a crowd but don't have a lot of time, this is one of my go-to recipes. Blending olives and mushrooms makes a tapenade-like spread that I can prepare ahead, and I love how the salty olives contrast with the mild pork tenderloin. I pair this dish with simple mashed potatoes or Roasted Pear and Cranberry Brussels Sprouts (page 172)—or both.

Jamaican Curry Chicken and Fried Dumplings

❧ Serves 4

❧ CURRY CHICKEN ❧

3 tablespoons canola oil

4 boneless, skinless chicken breasts, cut into ½- to 1-inch cubes

2 teaspoons kosher salt

1 teaspoon freshly ground black pepper

½ yellow onion, chopped

1 green onion, thinly sliced

2 thyme sprigs

2 garlic cloves, minced

2 to 4 tablespoons Jamaican-style hot yellow curry powder, such as Grace or Betapac, depending on your desired level of heat

2 Yukon gold potatoes, diced (about 3 cups)

1 tablespoon dark brown sugar

2 cups water

4 cups Steamed Jasmine Rice (page 168), for serving (optional)

❧ DUMPLINGS ❧

2 cups all-purpose flour

1 teaspoon baking powder

½ teaspoon kosher salt

4 tablespoons (½ stick) unsalted butter, cold and cubed

¼ cup cold water

1 cup canola oil, for frying

To make the curry chicken: Heat the oil in a medium pot or Dutch oven over medium-high heat. Add half of the chicken and season with 1 teaspoon of the salt and ½ teaspoon of the black pepper. Cook, stirring occasionally, until the chicken begins to brown, about 3 minutes. Transfer the chicken to a bowl and repeat with the remaining chicken, salt, and pepper. When the second batch is done cooking, return the first batch to the pot. Stir in the yellow onion, green onion, and thyme, lower the heat to medium, and cook, stirring occasionally, until the onion begins to soften, about 3 minutes.

continued on page 148 ᘐ

I know that I'm incredibly lucky to have grown up around great Jamaican cooks. But a lot of people have no idea what Jamaican food tastes like. This spicy curry is here to remedy the situation. I've kept things simple so this recipe can work on a weeknight, but it tastes even better the next day. If you really want to channel your inner Yardie (Caribbean expat), serve the chicken with Jamaican dumplings and fried plantains—and go overboard on the curry powder. If spicy curry isn't your thing, dial it back. (Some curry mixes are spicier than others.)

Jamaican Curry Chicken and Fried Dumplings, continued

Add the garlic and curry powder and stir well to coat all the chicken and onion pieces. Cook for 2 more minutes. Stir in the potatoes and brown sugar, pour in the water, and bring to a boil. Lower to a gentle simmer and cook until the potatoes are cooked through, about 15 minutes. Remove the thyme sprigs and keep the curry warm.

To make the dumplings: In a large bowl, whisk together the flour, baking powder, and salt. Add the cold butter and use your fingers or a fork to cut the butter into the flour until a crumbly mixture forms. Stir in the water and mix with your hands until the dumpling dough comes together. If the dough is too dry, add another 2 to 3 teaspoons water and continue mixing. Pinch off pieces of dough roughly the size of small golf balls and flatten them into discs. You should get about 12 discs.

In a large cast-iron skillet, heat the oil. Line a plate with paper towels and have a slotted spoon handy. To test if the oil is hot enough, put the end of a wooden spoon in the oil and see if bubbles form around it. (The ideal oil temperature is 350°F; feel free to check it with a deep-fry thermometer.)

In batches, fry the dumplings until golden brown, about 2 minutes per side. Drain on the paper towel–lined plate.

Spoon the curry onto plates or bowls and serve with the dumplings and a side of rice, if desired.

Fried Plantains

Plantains—or what we call "plan-tins" in Jamaica, ha!—must be super ripe before you fry them. Otherwise you won't get the sweet flavor and soft texture that make them so good. Most of the time, I find that plantains at the grocery store just aren't there yet. So, I put them in a brown paper bag, throw them in the dark part of my pantry, and leave them there for 2 or 3 days. *Voilà*, ripe plantains. To fry them, all you do is slice them up like bananas and deep-fry them in canola oil until they are deep golden brown on the outside and soft in the center. (Here I am, giving you tips like a true Yardie—my mom would be proud!)

Balsamic Lamb Chops

∽ Serves 4

8 small lamb rib chops
(about 1½ pounds)

1 tablespoon kosher salt

½ teaspoon freshly
ground black pepper

Leaves from 2 small
rosemary sprigs

1 cup balsamic vinegar
(preferably fig-infused)

¼ to ½ cup sugar
(depending on how sweet
your balsamic vinegar is)

Preheat an outdoor grill or have a cast-iron grill pan handy.

Season the lamb chops with the salt and pepper, then sprinkle with the rosemary leaves and massage the seasonings into the meat. (This helps the flavors seep into the lamb and release the aromas of the rosemary.) Let the lamb sit at room temperature while you make the balsamic sauce.

In a saucepan, heat the vinegar and ¼ cup sugar over medium-high heat. Bring to a boil, lower the heat to medium, and cook until the vinegar has reduced by half and is thick enough to coat the back of a spoon, about 9 minutes. If the vinegar tastes too sharp for your liking, stir in more sugar until it reaches a level you like.

If using a grill pan, preheat the pan over medium-high heat.

Grill the lamb chops until cooked through and dark grill marks appear, 3 to 5 minutes per side for medium-rare to medium. Let rest for 5 minutes before serving. Transfer to a platter and drizzle some balsamic vinegar sauce over the top. Serve extra at the table so people can help themselves.

Lamb chops are hearty and delicious, and my family— especially Stephen—loves them. To complement the rich flavor of the lamb, I like to make a sauce using a good balsamic vinegar, preferably one infused with fig. Of course, I have to sneak some sugar into the sauce, too. These chops are great with Roasted Pear and Cranberry Brussels Sprouts (page 172) or Herb-Roasted Potatoes with Lime (page 171).

Easy Pan Steaks

⚜ Serves 2 to 4

2 (1½-inch-thick)
filet mignon steaks
(about 8 ounces each)

Kosher salt

Freshly ground black pepper

2 tablespoons
salted butter

1 tablespoon extra-virgin
olive oil

2 rosemary sprigs

2 garlic cloves, peeled

Flaky sea salt, such as
Maldon, for serving
(optional)

⚜ Preheat the oven to 450°F. Season the steaks on both sides with salt and pepper.

Heat a large cast-iron skillet over medium-high heat until just smoking and add the butter and oil. When the butter has melted, add the steaks and let them sear for 3 minutes without moving (it is tempting to want to push the steaks around in the pan, but this will prevent them from getting that perfect caramelized crust).

Turn the steaks over, toss in the rosemary and garlic, and put the skillet in the oven for 5 minutes for medium-rare, or more depending on your preferred level of doneness (7 minutes in my oven makes for a perfect medium). Each additional 2 minutes should bring you to the next level of doneness. For serious accuracy, insert an instant-read meat thermometer into the center of the filet to test (medium-rare is about 140°F and medium is about 155°F). Remember, your steaks will continue to cook as they rest.

Using tongs, transfer the steaks to a cutting board. Now pay attention, because here is one of the most important steps: Let the steaks rest for at least 5 minutes after they are done. This allows the meat to relax and the juices to get reabsorbed into the meat.

To serve, either slice the steaks across the grain, or serve one per person. Offer Maldon salt at the table for an extra crunchy, salty bite.

These pan steaks are part of one of my family-favorite meals—steak and potatoes. Cooking steak in a cast-iron pan allows it to get a crisp caramelized crust. I throw in some butter, rosemary, and garlic to boost the flavor. For extra crunch, I like to sprinkle the finished steaks with Maldon sea salt. It is not the healthiest of dinners (whatever that means), but it's delicious, and sometimes that's all that matters. Serve the steaks with my Smoky "Un-Loaded" Potatoes (page 175).

Papa Alexander's Meat Loaf

⁓ Serves 6 to 8

½ cup ketchup, plus more for the pan and coating the meat loaf

2 teaspoons dark brown sugar, plus more for the pan

2 pounds 85% lean ground beef

⅔ cup finely chopped celery

⅔ cup finely chopped carrot

⅓ cup finely chopped green onion, plus 2 whole green onions, trimmed, for topping

2 or 3 garlic cloves, minced

2 large eggs, lightly beaten

1 tablespoon yellow mustard

1 tablespoon oyster sauce

½ to 1 tablespoon hot sauce

1 cup Italian-style breadcrumbs

1½ teaspoons minced fresh thyme

1 teaspoon kosher salt, plus more for seasoning

1 teaspoon freshly ground black pepper, plus more for seasoning

1 teaspoon dried thyme

1 teaspoon garlic powder

¼ teaspoon ground sage

⁓ Preheat the oven to 350°F. Oil a medium roasting pan (preferably one that comes with a lid) or a 9-by-13-inch baking pan. Coat the bottom of the pan with a few spoonfuls of ketchup and sprinkle with a spoonful or two of dark brown sugar.

Combine all the ingredients except for the whole green onions in a large bowl. Using your hands, mix and squish the ingredients together until evenly incorporated. It should be firm enough to hold the shape of a loaf.

Form the meat mixture into a loaf with tapered ends, like a small football. (Unlike a lot of meat loaf recipes, my dad's doesn't touch the sides of the roasting pan.) Place the loaf on top of the ketchup and brown sugar in the prepared pan. Using your finger, make a thin indented line lengthwise down the center of the loaf and make several lines across the loaf. (These will help hold the green onions and a layer of ketchup.)

Coat the meat loaf generously with more ketchup and season with salt and pepper. Lay the reserved green onions on top of the meat loaf in the shape of a cross, using the indentations to help hold them in place.

Cover the pan with a lid or aluminum foil and bake for 45 minutes. Uncover the pan and bake until the top of the meat loaf is golden brown and the internal temperature at the center reaches 160°F, about 15 more minutes. Set aside to cool for 10 minutes, then cut crosswise into thick slices and serve hot.

When we lived in Toronto, this is the one dish we could always count on my dad making, in our old-school speckled black roasting pan. And we could always count on it being delicious. You can swap out 1 pound of the ground beef for 1 pound of ground pork for a different flavor, if you like. For hot sauce, I like Tapatío or Crystal, but my dad says only Frank's RedHot will do. So use your favorite (but don't tell him). And for those of us (me) who like movie references: "Ma! The meat loaf!" (Ha!)

Mirin and Soy Steak with Sushi Rice

◦⧉ Serves 4

1 cup sushi rice

1¼ cups water, plus more for rinsing

¼ cup mirin

¼ cup low-sodium soy sauce

1 tablespoon dark brown sugar

2 tablespoons canola oil

1 pound filet mignon or other tender cut of beef, cut into 1-inch pieces

½ teaspoon kosher salt

½ teaspoon freshly ground black pepper

8 ounces cremini mushrooms, cut into quarters

1 medium yellow onion, sliced

½ teaspoon garlic powder

¼ cup sliced green onion (green parts only), for garnish

⧉ Put the rice in a fine-mesh strainer or colander and rinse a few times until the water runs relatively clear. Shake to remove excess water and transfer the rice to a medium pot.

Add 1¼ cups fresh water and bring to a boil over medium-high heat. Cover the pot, turn the heat to low, and cook for 10 minutes. Remove the pot from the heat and let it sit for 10 to 15 minutes to allow the rice to continue to steam.

In a small bowl, whisk together the mirin, soy sauce, and brown sugar.

Heat 1 tablespoon of the oil in a large skillet over high heat. Add the beef and season with salt and pepper. Cook for about 1 minute per side, just to get a light sear on the meat. Transfer to a plate. Add the remaining 1 tablespoon of oil and the mushrooms and onion to the skillet and season with the garlic powder. Sauté until the mushrooms just begin to soften, about 3 minutes. Return the beef and any juices to the pan and pour in the seasoning sauce. Cook the sauce down until the meat is warmed through and lightly glazed with the sauce. Be careful not to cook for too long or the meat will be dry—it's best when it's still pink in the center.

Fluff the rice with a fork and transfer it to a large serving bowl. Pour the meat, mushrooms, and all the sauce on top. Or divide the rice among four plates and spoon the meat, mushrooms, and sauce on top. Garnish with the green onions and serve.

I am a little obsessed with sushi rice. It's sticky and chewy and surprisingly fantastic with steak. This recipe is my take on what happens when you give steak and mushrooms a sushi make-over. You don't have to roll anything together, but you get all the benefits of the sweet mirin-soy flavors and the heartiness of beef. Serve it with Roasted Broccolini (page 176).

Stephen's Five-Ingredient Pasta

❧ Serves 4 to 6

12 ounces egg noodles

8 ounces chopped pancetta (about 1½ cups)

2 red bell peppers, seeded and diced

1 cup finely grated Parmesan

Generous handful of fresh basil leaves, larger leaves torn

❧ Bring a large pot of salted water to a boil. Add the noodles and cook according to the package directions.

Meanwhile, heat a large skillet over medium heat. Cook the pancetta until nice and crisp, about 5 minutes. Using a slotted spoon, transfer the pancetta to a bowl and pour off about half of the fat. (You should have about ¼ cup fat left in the pan.) Add the peppers and cook, tossing occasionally, until they are softened, about 5 minutes.

Drain the noodles, saving ½ cup of the pasta water, and return the noodles to the large pot. Stir in the crispy pancetta and the peppers. Add about ¼ cup of the reserved pasta water and stir in the cheese, adding more of the pasta water if the pasta looks dry. Stir in the basil right before serving.

Stephen was watching The Chew *when he saw Michael Symon cook up a quick pasta for a five-ingredient, five-minute challenge. A week or so later, it was his turn to make dinner, and he wanted to try out Michael's dish. It didn't go so well: He bought tomatoes instead of peppers and burned the egg noodles in the pot. But you know the motto: If at first you don't succeed, try, try again. Now he's a pro at making this dish, and it's become his signature. Any time he's in charge of dinner, it's pretty much guaranteed that this is what we'll be eating.*

SAUCES AND SIDES

Basil-Sage Pesto

Makes 1 heaping cup

2 packed cups fresh
basil leaves

¼ cup fresh sage leaves

4 garlic cloves, coarsely
chopped

½ cup grated Pecorino
Romano cheese

⅓ cup toasted pine nuts

1 cup extra-virgin olive oil

Kosher salt

Freshly ground black pepper

Combine all the ingredients in a blender or food processor and season with a couple of pinches each of salt and pepper. Blend until nearly smooth, about 30 seconds. Store any leftovers in an airtight container in the refrigerator for up to 1 week.

I started making pesto when Riley was still a tiny toddler. The first pizza she ever had was a gluten-free pesto pizza, and she loved it. Ever since then I've made pesto to put on pasta and fish, especially lighter kinds such as tilapia or sole. (Try it on the Salt-Baked Branzino on page 125.) It's great in the summer with a little fresh tomato. When serving this pesto, keep some fresh lemons on hand to brighten up the finished dish.

Parsley-Mint Sauce

⁓ Makes 1½ cups

1½ cups fresh flat-leaf parsley leaves

½ cup fresh mint leaves

2 green onions, coarsely chopped

2 or 3 garlic cloves, coarsely chopped

¾ cup extra-virgin olive oil

¼ cup water

Juice of 1 lemon (about ¼ cup)

2 tablespoons honey

¾ teaspoon kosher salt

⁓ Combine all the ingredients in a blender or food processor and blend until smooth.

It's hard not to be a fan of this light sauce, which counters the zing in my Grilled Spiced Chicken (page 134). I spoon it on everything from grilled fish to sandwiches and salads, and have even used it as a dip. It's great on grilled asparagus, but zucchini or any other green veggies are also fair game. Make it ahead (it will keep in an airtight container in the refrigerator for up to 1 week) and you have an easy weeknight meal in the works.

Cucumber Salad

Serves 4

1 English cucumber,
peeled

2 tablespoons red
wine vinegar

2 tablespoons minced
red onion

2 teaspoons sugar

½ teaspoon kosher salt

¼ teaspoon dried
chile flakes

Cut the cucumber in half lengthwise, then crosswise into ¼-inch-thick slices.

In a serving bowl, mix the vinegar, onion, sugar, salt, and chile flakes. Toss the cucumbers in the dressing and let them sit for at least 5 minutes to soak in the vinegar. Serve immediately, or refrigerate and serve within 4 hours.

This recipe pays homage to sweet, vinegary Jamaican cucumber salad. It's ideal for serving alongside spicy food, like Jerk Turkey (page 141), to cool you down. This salad is best served the day it's made; after that, the cucumber loses its crunch. For a make-ahead variation, swap out the cucumber for shredded cabbage and carrots and refrigerate it overnight. Then you'll have a Jamaican-style slaw, ready when you are.

The Best Mac and Cheese

❧ Serves 6 to 8

3 cups shredded aged or extra-sharp Cheddar cheese

4 tablespoons (½ stick) unsalted butter, cubed, at room temperature

1 tablespoon sugar

1 teaspoon ground mustard

½ teaspoon kosher salt

1 pound elbow macaroni

2½ cups whole milk

1 large egg

1 cup grated Parmesan cheese

4 ounces pancetta, finely diced (about 1 cup)

½ cup panko breadcrumbs

1 tablespoon minced fresh flat-leaf parsley

❧ Preheat the oven to 425°F. Butter a 9-by-13-inch baking pan.

In a large bowl, combine the Cheddar, butter cubes, sugar, ground mustard, and salt.

Bring a large pot of salted water to a boil over high heat. Add the macaroni and cook until al dente, a minute or so less than the recommended cooking time on the package. Drain well. While it's still hot, dump the macaroni into the Cheddar-butter mixture and toss to mix well.

Meanwhile, in a small saucepan, bring the milk to a bare simmer over medium heat. In a medium bowl, whisk the egg briefly to break it up. Temper the egg by drizzling ½ cup of the warm milk into the egg while whisking until incorporated. (This will prevent the egg from scrambling.) Mix the tempered egg and the remaining warm milk into the macaroni and stir well until everything is evenly coated.

Pour the contents of the bowl into the prepared baking pan, spreading the macaroni and sauce evenly.

In a medium bowl, toss together the Parmesan, pancetta, panko, and parsley. Sprinkle the crumble over the top of the macaroni. (This will create a yummy crust.)

Bake until the top is golden brown and bubbling and the pancetta is crispy, 25 to 30 minutes. Serve warm.

This mac and cheese is extra cheesy, including a generous amount of cheese on top. There's also a pinch of ground mustard to give it some depth, and an addictive pancetta "crumble" on top. To save some time, look for already chopped pancetta in the deli section of the grocery store. If you can't find it, buy strips of pancetta and chop them up yourself.

Steamed Jasmine Rice

❧ Serves 4

1½ cups jasmine rice

1¾ cups water,* plus more
for rinsing

Put the rice in a fine-mesh strainer or colander and rinse a few times until the water runs relatively clear. Shake to remove the excess water and transfer the rice to a medium pot.

Add 1¾ cups fresh water and bring to a boil over medium-high heat. Cover the pot, turn the heat to low, and cook for 10 minutes. Remove the pot from the heat and fluff the rice with a fork. Cover the pot and let it sit off the heat for 10 to 15 minutes to allow the rice to continue to steam.

*For the same quantity of brown rice, increase the water to 3½ cups.

I serve a side of jasmine rice as often as some might serve mashed potatoes. Because it can soak up flavors easily, it's the perfect match for so many main dishes I make, especially anything with an Asian or Jamaican influence. Some people are intimidated by cooking rice, but there's no need to worry about it. You can always use a rice cooker, but if that's too much of a commitment, make it on the stovetop with this recipe.

Herb-Roasted Potatoes with Lime

Serves 4

2 pounds small (1 to 1½ inches in diameter) multicolored or red "marble" potatoes, halved (or quartered if larger)

4 tablespoons (½ stick) unsalted butter, melted

2 tablespoons minced shallot

3 or 4 garlic cloves, minced

3 fresh thyme sprigs

1 fresh rosemary sprig

Kosher salt

Freshly ground black pepper

1 lime, halved

Preheat the oven to 425°F. Line a rimmed baking sheet with aluminum foil and oil lightly.

Put the potatoes in a large bowl and toss with the butter, shallot, garlic, thyme, and rosemary. Transfer the potatoes to the prepared baking sheet, season generously with salt and pepper, and bake until golden brown and crispy, 20 to 25 minutes, stirring once halfway through cooking. Remove the thyme and rosemary sprigs. Squeeze half of a lime on top, stir, and taste, adding more lime juice if desired. Serve warm.

So many dishes in this chapter are made even better with a side of these potatoes. *Making Mama Alexander's Brown Sugar Chicken (page 132), Soy-Citrus Salmon (119), or Salt-Baked Branzino (page 125)? Make these, too. The secret is the combination of tangy lime juice with savory shallot, garlic, and thyme.*

Roasted Pear and Cranberry Brussels Sprouts

❧ Serves 4

1½ pounds Brussels sprouts (about 30), halved

2 pears, cored and cut into 8 wedges each

½ cup finely chopped yellow onion

2 tablespoons extra-virgin olive oil

Kosher salt

Freshly ground black pepper

3 or 4 lemon wedges

1 tablespoon honey

¼ cup dried cranberries

❧ Preheat the oven to 450°F. Line a rimmed baking sheet with aluminum foil.

In a large bowl, combine the Brussels sprouts, pears, and onion and toss to coat with the olive oil. Season with a few pinches each of salt and pepper.

Transfer to the prepared baking sheet and bake until the Brussels sprouts are golden brown and have started to crisp and the pears have caramelized, 25 to 30 minutes, stirring once halfway through cooking.

Squeeze 3 of the lemon wedges over the pan and drizzle with the honey. Toss in the dried cranberries, mix everything well, and taste, adding another squeeze of lemon or more salt and pepper if desired. I promise this dish will not disappoint.

I can eat an entire bowl of these Brussels sprouts and still go back for seconds. It is a great side dish at dinner, especially in the fall and winter. The sweetness of the pear, the tartness of the dried cranberries, and the caramelized edges of the Brussels sprouts make for smiling faces around my family table.

For the best-tasting Brussels sprouts, bake them on a large rimmed baking sheet to ensure they have plenty of room to spread out. Crowding them into a small baking pan will cause them to steam, which won't let them get that crisp texture.

Spiced Butternut Squash Mash

❧ Serves 4 to 6

6 cups peeled, seeded, and cubed butternut squash

Kosher salt

6 tablespoons (¾ stick) salted butter, cubed

¼ cup milk (preferably whole)

¼ cup unsalted cashew butter

2 tablespoons dark brown sugar

1 tablespoon curry powder

1½ teaspoons garlic powder

1½ teaspoons onion powder

1 teaspoon freshly ground black pepper

¾ teaspoon ground nutmeg

Put the butternut squash in a large pot and pour in enough water to cover. Season with two large pinches of salt. Bring the water to a boil over high heat, then lower to a gentle simmer and cook until the squash is tender when pierced with a fork, about 15 minutes.

Drain the squash and return it to the pot. Using a potato masher, mash in the butter, milk, and cashew butter. When the squash is fairly smooth, mash in the brown sugar, curry powder, garlic powder, onion powder, black pepper, and nutmeg. You want the consistency to be smooth, but not baby-food smooth. Serve hot.

Spiced with curry powder, nutmeg, and pepper, this side dish is perfect with Jerk Turkey (page 141), but it's also a great alternative to plain mashed sweet potatoes served with any main course. I like how cashew butter complements the spices, giving the mash a richer flavor. It's becoming easier to find cashew butter at the store, but it's also not hard to make at home (with the help of a powerful blender). I put ¼ cup of raw, unsalted cashews in my Vitamix, crank it all the way up for about 20 seconds, and I'm done. For a deeper flavor, give the cashews a quick toast in a pan before blending.

Smoky "Un-Loaded" Potatoes

⟨ Serves 4

4 large red-skinned
potatoes, scrubbed
and cut into large cubes
(1½ to 2 pounds total)

Kosher salt

2 tablespoons cream
cheese, at room
temperature

½ cup grated smoked
Gruyère cheese

Freshly ground
black pepper

1 cup supersweet corn
kernels (from about 1 cob)

Chopped fresh chives, for
garnish (optional)

Put the potatoes in a
pot and cover with water.
Season with two large
pinches of salt. Bring the
water to a boil over high
heat, then lower to a simmer
and cook until the potatoes
are fork-tender, about
10 minutes. Drain well.

Transfer the potatoes to a
bowl while still hot. Add the
cream cheese and Gruyère
and briefly mash with a fork.
Season with salt and pepper
to taste, then gently fold in
the corn (don't overmix). Top
with the chives (if desired)
and serve.

I'm not big on baked potatoes and sour cream, but I do love
smoky, creamy mashed potatoes. So this is my version of
a loaded baked potato without the bacon or the sour cream…
or the baked potato, for that matter. Instead, a little smoked
Gruyère almost fools you into thinking there is bacon in there,
the cream cheese gives a rich, tangy flavor, and the corn keeps
the texture fun. (Be sure to use uncooked corn for the best
crunch factor.) I use a fork to mash the potatoes because it
leaves more irregular chunks of potato. Serve these potatoes
with Easy Pan Steaks (page 153) for a steakhouse meal
at home.

Roasted Broccolini

⊰ Serves 4

2 bunches broccolini, trimmed

2 garlic cloves, crushed with the flat side of a knife

Kosher salt

Freshly ground black pepper

3 tablespoons extra-virgin olive oil

Preheat the oven to 450°F. Line a rimmed baking sheet with aluminum foil and lightly oil it.

Scatter the broccolini and garlic on the prepared baking sheet. Season with salt and pepper and drizzle the oil over the top. Roast until the florets are nicely browned and the stalks have started to become tender but are still firm when pierced with a fork, about 8 minutes. Serve the broccolini (and garlic, if desired) warm.

To my way of thinking, the ideal vegetable dish to serve with Mirin and Soy Steak with Sushi Rice (page 156) or Salt-Baked Branzino (page 125) is roasted broccolini, broccoli's more sophisticated cousin. That it's so easy to make is a bonus: The long, skinny stems roast up quickly in a hot oven. If you want to dress it up more, add a drizzle of balsamic vinegar or a squeeze of lemon juice when finished.

Q&A with Stephen

A Has your palate changed since you were in college? Have I helped?

S You have aided in that 100 percent. It's what you advise me to order when we go out to eat. It's how you get me to try everything from sushi to some random ingredient that I would never have thought would be good. Actually, I still don't quite like bacon-wrapped dates, but I eat a lot more of them now. You are always trying to get me to try them.

A Remember the chai latte incident when we were first dating? Do you want to tell your side of the story?

S I knew she was coming over. I ran across the street to Starbucks and bought two big—venti?—chai tea lattes. In my family's kitchen, we had these huge canisters on the counter where you could put things like almonds and flour. I hid the chai tea latte cups in the empty dog food canister. You came over, started talking, yada yada, and I said, "Do you want a chai tea latte?" I acted like I was putting some ingredients together, and then I distracted you and poured the chai tea lattes into the pot.

A And then?

S My sister ratted me out.

A She said, "Why do you have the dog food container out?"

S Those "homemade" chai tea lattes cost me $9.

A What's your favorite dish that I cook?

S Lamb chops with balsamic dressing. And bread pudding.

A What's the least favorite?

S I can't think of anything. Well, anything with chocolate I won't eat. Or that one time you put garlic in the eggs. For breakfast. That was awful!

A Yeah, I don't know why I did that. You're truly my guinea pig.

Drinks

{ FOR DAYTIME AND
GROWN-UP TIME

I'**LL NEVER FORGET** my 21st birthday. Stephen decided to take me out to the Slanted Door, a beautiful Vietnamese restaurant in San Francisco's Ferry Building. Turning 21 was a big deal for me. Like most of us, I admit that I had had a couple of sips of wine here and there before I turned 21. But honestly, I waited until that birthday for a real grown-up beverage.

I was excited. I ordered a cocktail. It looked amazing. I tasted it. And I *hated* it. I ordered another. And I hated that, too. This went on until at the end of it, there were ten drinks on the table. Stephen was annoyed, but my palate at 21 was just not developed enough to appreciate any of these great drinks. I did finally find one I liked, an amaretto sour. For the next two years, it was amaretto sours and the occasional glass of Moscato—and that was all I'd take a chance on. Talk about sugar!

Today, I'm happy to report that I've moved on. While I still do love the occasional amaretto sour, my appreciation for other options has grown a lot. I have developed a love for not only many different kinds of cocktails but also a variety of wines. Now I get it.

What helped me expand my appreciation for cocktails was when I started making them myself and learned to have fun discovering new liqueurs—like elderflower (see page 196). These days, I also like knowing what's going into the glass so I can control the quality, quantity, and sugar level. When I became pregnant, I switched to making mocktails. Some cocktails, especially lighter ones that are flavored with citrus or herbs like lavender, make great nonalcoholic options—just remove the booze and top off with more tonic or club soda.

This chapter isn't just about being an amazing bartender, though. I also love making Mango Lemonade (page 191), Island Green Smoothies (page 187), or even a nice, warm cup of Almond Milk Chai Latte (page 183). It's really all about balance and making sure there are options for everyone in the group, no matter their age or preference.

Here's to refreshing ideas!

Almond Milk Chai Lattes

Serves 4

❦ ALMOND MILK ❧

1½ cups raw almonds

3⅔ cups water, plus more for soaking

1 vanilla bean, slit open and seeds scraped out

4 Medjool dates, pitted and coarsely chopped

¼ teaspoon ground nutmeg

❦ CHAI LATTE ❧

3 cups water

6 English breakfast tea bags

1 cinnamon stick

1 piece star anise

6 green cardamom pods

½ teaspoon ground ginger

½ teaspoon ground nutmeg

Pinch of ground allspice

2 tablespoons sugar

2 tablespoons sweetened condensed milk

To make the almond milk: Put the almonds in a bowl and cover with about 1 inch of water. Soak overnight at room temperature. Drain well. Transfer the almonds to a blender, along with the vanilla seeds, dates, nutmeg, and 3½ cups fresh water, and blend until smooth. This usually takes 1½ to 3 minutes, depending on the blender. Put a nut milk bag or a fine-mesh strainer lined with cheesecloth over a bowl or large liquid measuring cup. Pour the nut blend through the bag, squeezing the bag or pushing down on the almond grounds from time to time to extract all of the liquid. You should have nearly 3 cups.

To make the chai lattes: In a small pot, bring the water to a simmer. Add the tea bags, spices, and sugar and simmer gently for 5 minutes. Strain into a heatproof liquid measuring cup, pressing on the tea bags to extract all the flavor. Meanwhile, warm up four mugs with hot water.

continued on page 184

Chai lattes always remind me of when Stephen and I first started dating. Back then he nearly fooled me into believing that he knew how to make them from scratch (see page 178 for the whole story). Years later, I decided to find a way to make them myself. It turns out that it's not so hard—plus, making them at home allows me to customize the spices and the type of milk. Feel free to make this recipe your own. I've used almond milk, but dairy milk is fine, too.

Before making almond milk, be sure to soak the almonds overnight. Plan on having a nut milk bag (sold at natural grocery stores) or a fine-mesh strainer lined with cheesecloth for straining the almonds. And if chai lattes aren't your thing, mix a little cocoa powder into the almond milk instead.

Almond Milk Chai Lattes, continued

In the same pot, add 1 cup of the almond milk and the condensed milk and heat gently over medium-low heat, whisking occasionally, until hot. (Avoid scorching the bottom of the pot.) Pour in the tea, frothing with a whisk if you choose. Taste and add more almond milk if desired. Empty the mugs of hot water and pour the tea into the mugs. Serve hot.

Ginger Tea

⅋ Serves 4

6 cups water

2 tablespoons chopped
fresh ginger

6 whole cloves

1 cinnamon stick

¼ cup freshly squeezed
lemon juice

Honey

In a medium saucepan, bring the water, ginger, cloves, and cinnamon to a boil. Lower to a gentle simmer for at least 5 minutes or up to 15 minutes, depending on how potent you want the ginger flavor. Stir in the lemon juice, then strain into a heatproof pitcher or teapot. Stir in a spoonful or two of honey.

Warm four mugs with hot water. Empty out the mugs and pour in the tea. Put the honey on the table in case anyone wants to make theirs sweeter.

Jamaicans love tea—ginger tea in particular. My family seems to think it's the remedy for every problem. "You have cramps?" Drink some tea. "You have a headache?" Drink some tea. "Your boyfriend dumped you?" Drink some tea. In all seriousness, though, this homemade herbal tea does soothe the soul. It gets bonus points for filling the house with a delicious aroma of spices.

Island Green Smoothie

Serves 2 to 3

1 cup diced fresh
pineapple

3 loosely packed cups
baby spinach

1½ cups coconut water

Blend all the ingredients
until smooth, then pour into
tall glasses and serve. This is
just delicious!

Let's just say that there's a certain smoothie chain that
Stephen can't get enough of. So I figured a while ago that
it would probably be a good idea to learn how to make
smoothies at home. It gives me peace of mind knowing what
is in each batch. Stephen likes his smoothies on the sweeter
side, so I came up with this tropical smoothie with fresh, sweet
pineapple especially for him. I love adding chia seeds to mine
or a protein boost, but I leave them out of his.

Holiday Smoothie

୫ Serves 2

2 ripe bananas, sliced
(and frozen, if desired,
for more of an ice cream
consistency)

4 Medjool dates, pitted
and coarsely chopped

1½ cups almond milk
(For extra credit, make
your own! See page 183
for instructions.)

2 teaspoons honey

Pinch of ground
cardamom

Pinch of ground allspice

Blend all the ingredients
until smooth, then pour into
tall glasses and serve.

This smoothie tastes like ice cream! Sweetened with dates and a little bit of honey, it blends up to smooth, creamy perfection. The spices make it smell amazing, too. If you're not into eggnog but don't want to miss out on the holiday fun, I consider this smoothie a really good alternative. Cheers to the holidays—or any day, really.

Mango Lemonade

✧ Serves 4 to 6

1 mango, peeled,
pitted, and chopped
(about 1½ cups)

¾ cup sugar

4 cups water

1 cup freshly squeezed
lemon juice

1 teaspoon bitters,
such as Angostura

✧ In a blender, blend the mango, ¼ cup of the sugar, and a splash of water until smooth. This will make the puree for the lemonade.

In a pitcher, combine the water, lemon juice, bitters, and the remaining ½ cup sugar. Stir until the sugar dissolves. Mix in the puree. Serve over ice in tall glasses.

This is lemonade with a twist: I add a few dashes of bitters to give it an aromatic, not-too-sweet edge. While I add pureed mango in this recipe, you can create a variety of flavors by using other fruit. Strawberry, blackberry, and watermelon are all fantastic. If the fruit is very sweet, you may wish to add less sugar (or no sugar at all) to the fruit puree. When entertaining, you can offer a bunch of purees and let your guests mix whatever they want into their lemonade. Poured over ice on a hot day, it's hard to beat as a thirst quencher.

Virgin Mule

Serves 4

½ cup sugar

½ cup water

Handful of fresh mint
leaves, plus a few
for garnish

Splash of pure
vanilla extract

4 limes, halved

6 cups ginger beer

First, make the mint simple syrup. In a small saucepan, bring the sugar, water, mint, and vanilla to a boil over high heat. Lower the heat to a simmer and cook until the sugar has dissolved completely, about 1 minute. Let cool to room temperature, then strain into a glass measuring cup.

For each mocktail, squeeze the juice from 1 lime into a serving glass or mug. Add 2 tablespoons mint simple syrup and stir. Add some ice and pour in 1½ cups ginger beer. Stir again and serve, garnished with a few mint leaves.

Throughout my first pregnancy, I craved a Moscow mule. So while everyone else was enjoying this cocktail, I would order the mocktail version of it—the virgin mule. Made with a minty simple syrup, this drink is so light and refreshing that you almost don't miss the real thing. The simple syrup is also a great way to use up mint that's starting to wilt. To go all out, serve it the traditional way in chilled copper mugs. Some brands of ginger beer are sweeter than others. To cut down sweetness, mix it with a little sparkling water.

Rosemary Grapefruit Cocktail

Serves 4

¼ cup sugar

¼ cup water

7 rosemary sprigs

1 cup freshly squeezed
grapefruit juice

1 cup sparkling water or
club soda

6 tablespoons rosemary
simple syrup

8 ounces vodka,
such as Tito's

First, make the rosemary simple syrup. In a small saucepan, bring the sugar, water, and 3 rosemary sprigs to a boil over medium-high heat. Lower the heat to a simmer and cook until the sugar has dissolved completely, about 1 minute. Let cool to room temperature, then remove the rosemary.

In a pitcher, stir together the grapefruit juice and the sparkling water.

For each cocktail, fill a glass with a handful of ice and add a rosemary sprig. In a cocktail shaker, stir together 2 ounces vodka with 1½ tablespoons rosemary simple syrup. Pour the contents of the shaker into the glass and top with ½ cup of the grapefruit sparkling water. Serve.

Cocktails are a great place to play around with presentation. That doesn't mean that you can put anything in the glass, though! I like to garnish this cocktail with rosemary because it clues you in to what flavor might be in the glass. While this recipe calls for 1 cup each of fresh grapefruit juice and sparkling water, you can use 2 cups of a good-quality grapefruit soda, like San Pellegrino, instead.

Lavender Elderflower Cocktail

⅋ Serves 4

¼ cup sugar

¼ cup water

3 strips lemon zest

½ cup freshly squeezed
lemon juice

4 fresh lavender
sprigs or 2 teaspoons
dried lavender

6 ounces vodka,
such as Tito's

4 ounces elderflower
liqueur, such as
St-Germain

✤ First, make the lemon simple syrup. In a small saucepan, bring the sugar, water, and lemon zest to a boil over medium-high heat. Lower the heat to a simmer and cook until the sugar has dissolved completely, about 1 minute. Let cool to room temperature, then remove the lemon zest.

For each cocktail, fill a tall glass with ice. Muddle together 2 tablespoons lemon juice and 1 lavender sprig (or ½ teaspoon dried lavender). This will release the essence of the lavender. Pour in 1 tablespoon lemon simple syrup, 1½ ounces vodka, and 1 ounce elder-flower liquor. Add a handful of ice and shake. Strain the cocktail into the glass and serve.

Here's the real story behind this cocktail: I was at the store and wanted to make a new cocktail. I picked up the prettiest bottle—I'm a sucker for that kind of stuff—and that's how I ended up with St-Germain elderflower liqueur. I had no idea what elderflower liqueur was, but I knew the taste: The first time you taste it you think, wow, it smells like lychee fruit. It's incredibly aromatic without being too sweet. I like to mix it into any sort of cocktail with a floral edge, which is why lavender seemed to be a natural addition. Fresh lavender grows all over California (and is usually on display at local farmers' markets), but if it's hard to find, dried lavender works, too.

Meyer Lemon Bourbon Cocktail

Makes 4 cocktails

8 ounces bourbon

8 tablespoons freshly squeezed lemon juice (preferably from Meyer lemons)

4 teaspoons pure maple syrup

Cointreau

1 vanilla bean, cut into quarters

To make each cocktail, in a cocktail shaker, combine 2 ounces bourbon, 2 tablespoons lemon juice, 1 teaspoon maple syrup, a splash of Cointreau, and a quarter of a vanilla bean. Add ice, shake, and strain into a glass.

This is the West Coast answer to a whisky cocktail (Meyer lemons), with a dash of Canada in there (maple syrup). A vanilla bean adds a little sweetness, but I cut it in quarters and I don't scoop out the seeds, so the vanilla flavor isn't too strong.

Harvest Sangria

⟨ Serves 4

¼ packed cup dark brown sugar

¼ cup water

6 whole cloves

1 apple, such as Honeycrisp, cored and chopped

4 ounces spiced rum (I prefer Captain Morgan)

8 ounces full-bodied red wine, such as Syrah, chilled

1 (12-ounce) bottle hard apple cider, such as Crispin or Angry Orchard, chilled

¼ teaspoon ground cinnamon

⟨ First, make the spiced simple syrup. In a small saucepan, bring the brown sugar, water, and cloves to a boil over medium-high heat. Lower the heat to a simmer and cook, stirring frequently to avoid burning the sugar, until the liquid turns into a thick, dark syrup, 2 to 3 minutes. Let cool to room temperature, then spoon out the cloves.

In a cocktail shaker or bowl, muddle the apple pieces and rum together, mashing and breaking up the apple pieces. Strain the rum into a carafe or pitcher, pressing gently on the apple solids to get as much liquid as you can. Add the spiced simple syrup and stir until the syrup has incorporated. Stir in the wine, apple cider, and cinnamon.

To serve, put ice in four glasses and pour the sangria over the ice.

I love classic sangria. The sweet, fruity flavor, the chunks of ripe fruit, the way it creeps up on you during a summer day.... The only limitation with sangria is that it's mostly served in the summer. To work around that, I made a spiced version that is cool-weather friendly. Even though it's still served over ice, the flavors of cinnamon and cloves warm the soul. Of course, wine warms you up, too, but that's not what I'm getting at here.

You can mix everything ahead of time, but leave out the hard cider until right before serving so it doesn't lose its carbonation. Serve ice in the glasses and not the pitcher to avoid diluting the sangria. If you think your friends are going to want seconds (and they just might), consider doubling this recipe.

Sweets

Regardless of the dining location or event, I'm the girl who is looking for—and asking about—dessert before drinks have been ordered. While I'm not sure how or when it started, there is no denying that I have an extremely mean sweet tooth. It shows up all the time in the way I cook savory food—as you can tell by my favorite dish from my mom, Mama Alexander's Brown Sugar Chicken (page 132). But it goes bananas when I get to dessert.

Stephen is well aware of this preference of mine. When he is traveling for road games, he has a habit of texting me a picture of the dessert menu. He guesses what I would pick. And he always, always gets it right. I'd say the answer is chocolate more than 50 percent of the time. Strangely enough, I am the only person in my immediate family who loves chocolate.

None of this means that I need my sweets to be complicated. The desserts in this chapter are all easy to make, especially the Rum and Chocolate Banana Bread (page 206) and the Amaretto Pound Cake with Lemon Glaze (page 204). And if you want to finish the meal with a bang, make Bananas Foster (page 212) and flambé the bananas in front of your friends—lighting a pan on fire is always a sure way to get people to remember the meal.

Here's to sweet dreams!

Amaretto Pound Cake with Lemon Glaze

❧ Makes 1 (4-by-8-inch) cake

❧ POUND CAKE ❧

Confectioners' sugar, for dusting

1½ cups all-purpose flour

2 teaspoons baking powder

1 teaspoon kosher salt

1 packed cup dark brown sugar

3 large eggs, at room temperature, lightly beaten

1 cup plain whole-milk Greek yogurt

½ cup extra-virgin olive oil or canola oil

⅓ cup freshly squeezed lemon juice

2 tablespoons amaretto

1 teaspoon pure vanilla extract

1 teaspoon bitters, such as Angostura

2 teaspoons grated lemon zest

❧ GLAZE ❧

1 cup confectioners' sugar

2 tablespoons freshly squeezed lemon juice

½ teaspoon bitters, such as Angostura

❧ To make the pound cake: Preheat the oven to 350°F. Oil a 4-by-8-inch loaf pan and dust with confectioners' sugar.

In a small bowl, whisk together the flour, baking powder, and salt.

In a larger bowl, whisk together the brown sugar, eggs, yogurt, oil, lemon juice, amaretto, vanilla, bitters, and zest. Using a spatula, gently mix the dry ingredients into the wet ingredients until smooth.

Pour the batter into the prepared loaf pan and bake until a toothpick inserted into the center comes out clean, 50 to 60 minutes. Let it cool for about 10 minutes, then unmold and cool completely on a wire rack.

To make the glaze: In a bowl, whisk together the confectioners' sugar, lemon juice, and bitters until smooth and creamy. Once the cake has cooled to room temperature, pour the glaze over the top of the cake. Slice and serve.

This pound cake is the perfect combination of sweet and savory. Its dense texture and light fragrant flavors of amaretto and lemon combine for the perfect way to end the evening. My family can't keep it in the kitchen for more than a couple of hours because it gets devoured by the big and little fingers in my household.

Rum and Chocolate Banana Bread

ᦾ Makes 1 (4-by-8-inch) loaf

1 packed cup plus
1 tablespoon dark
brown sugar

2 cups all-purpose flour

¼ cup ground flaxseed

1 teaspoon baking soda

¼ teaspoon kosher salt

6 tablespoons (¾ stick)
unsalted butter,
at room temperature

3 ripe bananas

1 large egg, at room
temperature, lightly beaten

½ cup whole milk,
at room temperature

¼ cup dark rum

1 tablespoon pure
vanilla extract

½ cup dark
chocolate chips

ᦾ Preheat the oven to 350°F. Coat a 4-by-8-inch loaf pan with nonstick cooking spray and sprinkle the bottom of the pan with 1 tablespoon brown sugar. (When the bread bakes it will form a deliciously sweet crust.)

In a small bowl, whisk together the flour, flaxseed, baking soda, and salt.

In a larger bowl, mash together the butter and bananas with a potato masher until smooth. Whisk in the remaining 1 cup brown sugar, egg, milk, rum, and vanilla.

Add the flour mixture and chocolate chips to the banana mixture and gently stir until the dry ingredients are just incorporated. Pour the batter into the prepared pan and bake until a toothpick inserted into the center of the bread comes out clean, 60 to 65 minutes. Let cool for about 10 minutes, then unmold and cool completely on a wire rack. Slice and serve.

I love a good banana bread, but even a classic can get boring. The solution: Make it with a full-bodied dark rum and dark chocolate. So let's welcome this new classic to the fold. For banana bread, I like to go low-tech: A fork works just fine for mixing.

Citrus–Olive Oil Cake

ꝫ Makes 1 (8-inch) cake

Confectioners' sugar,
for dusting

1½ cups all-purpose flour

2 teaspoons
baking powder

¼ teaspoon kosher salt

1 cup sugar

1 cup extra-virgin olive oil

3 large eggs, lightly beaten

¼ cup whole milk

½ teaspoon pure
vanilla extract

¼ teaspoon pure
almond extract

2 tablespoons grated
grapefruit zest (from about
1 grapefruit)

1 tablespoon grated
orange zest (from about
1 orange)

1 tablespoon orange juice

ఞ Preheat the oven to 350°F. Oil an 8-inch round cake pan and dust with confectioners' sugar.

In a small bowl, whisk together the flour, baking powder, and salt.

In a larger bowl, whisk together the sugar, oil, eggs, milk, vanilla and almond extracts, grapefruit zest, and orange zest and juice. Using a spatula, gently mix the dry ingredients into the wet ingredients until smooth.

Pour the batter into the prepared pan and bake until a toothpick inserted into the center comes out clean, about 40 minutes. Let cool in the pan for about 10 minutes, then unmold and cool completely on a wire rack. Cut into wedges and serve.

I could go on and on about how much I love olive trees. I even have olive trees growing in my yard—and that's just the beginning of my obsession. So, it didn't take much convincing for me to try making a dessert with olive oil, and citrus is a natural pairing. I like to serve this cake with plain whipped cream and basil leaves for garnish. Or simply dust the top with confectioners' sugar and call it a day.

White Chocolate Bread Pudding

Serves 6

2 cups milk (preferably whole), warmed slightly to take the chill off

½ cup cane sugar or granulated sugar

1 large egg, lightly beaten

Splash of pure vanilla extract

Splash of pure almond extract

1 teaspoon ground cinnamon

6 croissants, torn into large pieces

1 cup white chocolate chips

Vanilla ice cream, for serving (optional)

1 recipe Bananas Foster (page 212), for serving

Preheat the oven to 400°F. Butter an 8-inch square baking dish.

In a large bowl, whisk together the milk and sugar, allowing the sugar to dissolve a bit. Whisk in the egg, vanilla and almond extracts, and cinnamon. Fold in the croissants and chocolate chips and let sit for a few minutes until the croissants have absorbed most of the milk.

Pour the mixture into the prepared dish, ensuring that the ingredients are evenly distributed. Bake until the pudding is set, about 30 minutes. Cool for at least 15 minutes before cutting into squares.

To serve the bread pudding, I go all out with a scoop of ice cream and a generous spoonful of Bananas Foster.

I am a huge dark chocolate fan. This is not so for Riley and Stephen, who can do without. But even I have to admit that white chocolate really works in this bread pudding. You get those creamy bites of chocolate in each bite. My brother-in-law, Seth, is now a fan. It's one of the ways we get him to drive down from Sacramento to visit us. This bread pudding happens to be a great make-ahead dish and can be easily reheated in the oven. What puts it over the top is the Bananas Foster (page 212).

Pumpkin Squares

1 cup (2 sticks) unsalted butter

2½ cups all-purpose flour

1 teaspoon baking powder

½ teaspoon baking soda

¾ teaspoon kosher salt

1½ teaspoons ground cinnamon

½ teaspoon ground nutmeg

½ teaspoon ground ginger

Pinch of ground allspice

1½ packed cups dark brown sugar

2 large eggs, lightly beaten

1 (15-ounce) can pumpkin puree (not pumpkin pie filling)

1 teaspoon pure vanilla extract

Coarse sugar, such as turbinado, for sprinkling on top (optional)

In a saucepan, melt the butter over medium-low heat and cook until the milk solids have fallen to the bottom of the pot and have started to turn golden brown and smell like toasted nuts, 10 minutes or longer depending on how cold the butter is to start.

Pour the butter into a large heatproof bowl and refrigerate, stirring occasionally, until the butter has cooled but is still liquid, about 20 minutes. It's okay if it solidifies along the sides of the bowl.

Preheat the oven to 350°F. Butter an 8-inch square baking pan. Line the bottom with parchment paper and butter the paper. Dust lightly with flour and shake out the excess.

In a medium bowl, whisk together the flour, baking powder, baking soda, salt, and spices.

Whisk the brown sugar into the bowl with the browned butter, making sure to scrape in any solidified butter from the sides of the bowl. Whisk in the eggs, followed by the pumpkin and the vanilla. With a rubber spatula, fold in the flour (it's okay if the batter seems a little thick) and mix until smooth.

Spread the batter into the prepared pan, smoothing the top with the spatula. Sprinkle coarse sugar on top if desired. Bake until a toothpick inserted into the center of the cake comes out clean, 55 minutes to 1 hour. Let cool to room temperature before cutting into 16 squares.

I still remember the menu from the first dinner I had with my in-laws—especially the dessert. These pumpkin squares have since become something of a family tradition during the fall, but I was looking for a new way to combine those same flavors. This version is filled with some of my favorite things—brown sugar (of course) and baking spices. For a little more richness, I brown the butter first, then let it cool before mixing the batter.

Bananas Foster

⤳ Serves 6

8 tablespoons (1 stick) unsalted butter

1 packed cup dark brown sugar

3 or 4 bananas, sliced crosswise

¼ cup spiced rum

Splash of heavy cream (optional)

⤳ Melt the butter in a large skillet over medium-high heat. When the butter is bubbly, sprinkle in the brown sugar and stir to combine. Return to a simmer and add the bananas, tossing to coat and warm through.

Pour in the rum and tip the pan toward the burner to encourage the rum to flambé, or catch fire. Or, if you're cooking on an electric or induction burner, light a long lighter or match and carefully hold it near the surface of the sauce to flambé. The flame cooks off the alcohol. If the sauce looks a little broken, with the butter separating from the sugar, add a splash of cream to help bring it back together. Serve immediately.

I think of this dessert trick as one of my signatures. What's not to like about lighting a pan on fire? It's flashy and fun to do when friends come over. Plus, it's absolutely amazing over my White Chocolate Bread Pudding (page 210).

Cast-Iron "Fruit Cake"

☙ Makes 1 (10-inch) cake

1 box favorite yellow cake mix (I like Duncan Hines), plus any ingredients needed for the mix

2 tablespoons unsalted butter

½ packed cup dark brown sugar

1 pint blackberries

1 cup diced pineapple

Leaves from 2 thyme sprigs

Vanilla ice cream, for serving

Preheat the oven to 350°F.

Prepare the cake mix batter as directed on the package and set aside.

In a 12-inch cast-iron skillet, melt the butter over medium heat and stir in the brown sugar. When the sugar has dissolved, stir in the berries, pineapple, and thyme. Mix until the brown sugar begins to bubble, about 2 minutes. Remove the skillet from heat.

Pour the cake batter into the skillet and bake until a toothpick inserted into the center comes out clean, about 30 minutes. Scoop the cake directly from the pan while still warm and serve with vanilla ice cream.

So, let's get real: This is something of a cheater recipe because it uses a box of cake mix. Still, I love this recipe because not only is it foolproof (after all, it's pretty hard to mess up a boxed mix), but it's a good trick to have when you need to make a dessert and are pressed for time. The finished product is like an upside-down cake served right-side up.

Deep-Fried Oreos

⅜ Makes about 30 cookies

1 (10-ounce) bottle instant
pancake batter (I use
Bisquick Shake 'n Pour)

Canola oil

1 package Oreo Double
Stuf cookies

Pour the pancake batter
into a bowl.

In a 4-quart saucepan or
Dutch oven, heat 2 inches of
oil (5 to 6 cups oil, depending on the pan). Line a
rimmed baking sheet with
paper towels and have a
slotted spoon handy. To test
if the oil is hot enough, put
the end of a wooden spoon
in the oil and see if bubbles
form around it. (The ideal oil
temperature is about 370°F;

feel free to check it with a
deep-fry thermometer.)

Dip each Oreo into the
batter so it's submerged.
Lift the Oreo out and
shake off any excess bat-
ter. Working in batches to
avoid crowding the pan, fry
the Oreos, flipping them
over halfway through, until
golden brown, about
1 minute. Drain on the paper
towel–lined baking sheet
and serve while still hot.

This recipe is 1,000 percent overindulgent, but there is a
time and a place for everything. I started to make my own
so I could enjoy this county-fair classic in the comfort of my
own home. You just can't go wrong with this one.

Key Lime Pie with Cinnamon Toast Crunch Crust

⋦ Serve 8 to 10

⋦ CRUST ⋩

1 (16.2-ounce) box
Cinnamon Toast
Crunch cereal

12 tablespoons (1½ sticks)
unsalted butter, melted

¼ cup packed dark brown
sugar

⋦ FILLING ⋩

6 cups sweetened
condensed milk

1 cup sour cream

1 cup freshly squeezed
Key lime juice

1 tablespoon grated
Key lime zest

*Note: regular limes work
fine. #NotBougie*

⋦ WHIPPED CREAM ⋩

2 cups heavy
whipping cream

2 tablespoons
confectioners' sugar

1 teaspoon pure
vanilla extract

1 tablespoon grated
Key lime zest

To make the crust:
Preheat the oven to 350°F.

In a food processor, pulse together the cereal, butter, and brown sugar until crumbly. Pack the crust into the bottom of a 9-by-13-inch baking pan, leaving the sides clean. Bake until the crust is lightly toasted, about 10 minutes.

To make the filling: While the crust bakes, in a bowl, whisk together the condensed milk, sour cream, lime juice, and lime zest. As soon as the crust comes out of the oven, carefully pour in the filling and place it back in the oven until the filling starts to set, about 10 minutes. Carefully remove the pie from the oven and let it cool to room temperature. Refrigerate the pie until chilled all the way through, at least 1 hour, though overnight is best.

To make the whipped cream: Combine the cream, sugar, vanilla, and lime zest in a bowl and beat with a whisk or an electric mixer until the cream forms soft peaks when the whisk is lifted out of the bowl. (Or use a stand mixer with the whisk attachment—this will make things go much faster, so watch it carefully.) Spoon the whipped cream on top of the pie, then cut into squares and serve.

I've mentioned already that chocolate is my dessert of choice. But it is definitely not Stephen's. Whenever we go out to eat, if there is Key lime pie on the menu, he is ordering it 99.9 percent of the time. When I wanted to put my own twist on it, I thought why not spice things up with cinnamon? A crust made with Cinnamon Toast Crunch was the answer.

Scrubs...

Lemon

Coffee

Brown Sugar
Vanilla

Pretty (Great) Extras

AFTER I HAD RILEY, I turned into the crazy eco lady. Everything had to be homemade. It started easily enough—rubbing coconut oil in my hair. But then it extended to making body scrubs. I'm still a little bit like that, but I've relaxed—*a lot*—since Ryan came along. You know that commercial when a new mom is giving everyone hand sanitizer for the first baby and then the second one comes along and she's playing in the mud and everything is fine? It's been a little like that.

Still, there is something to be said for being able to make your own beauty products. I wanted to take food beyond simply cooking. If healthy food can benefit your body by eating it, it can probably benefit your body on the outside, too. And I like the idea that I'm using up things like coffee grounds that would otherwise hit the compost heap.

Here's to making your own pretty extras!

Lemon and Sea Salt Scrub

❧ Makes about 1 cup

1 cup coarse sea salt

2 or 3 large strips lemon rind

¼ cup extra-virgin olive oil

Put the salt in a pint-size mason jar and pack in the rind. Stir in the olive oil and cap the jar. Rub it into your skin while in the shower (avoid the bottoms of your feet so you don't slip). Be sure to moisturize after. (Coconut oil does the trick for that.)

The scrub can be kept in the refrigerator for up to 2 weeks or in the bathroom for up to 1 week. Any longer and you'll have preserved lemon—which is better for cooking than using as a scrub!

Chefs love curing lemon rinds in salt to make preserved lemons, but I mix the two to make an aromatic body scrub.

Coffee Scrub

❧ Makes about 1 cup

1 cup used coffee grounds

3 to 4 tablespoons extra-virgin olive or coconut oil

In a bowl, mix the coffee grinds and oil to create a paste-like scrub. Rub it into your skin while in the shower (avoid the bottoms of your feet so you don't slip). Be sure to moisturize after. (Coconut oil does the trick for that.)

Use those old coffee grounds to benefit your body (especially the pesky thigh area). Coffee applied topically to the skin has been known to increase circulation and blood flow—this means less cellulite and tighter brighter skin! No brainer.

Brown Sugar–Vanilla Body Scrub

֍ Makes about 1 cup

1 packed cup dark
brown sugar

3 tablespoons coconut oil

1 vanilla bean, partially
split lengthwise

֍ In a pint-size mason jar, mix the brown sugar and coconut oil. Put the vanilla bean in the sugar, split end in first, and cap the jar. Rub it into your skin while in the shower (avoid the bottoms of your feet so you don't slip). Be sure to moisturize after. (Coconut oil does the trick for that.)

The scrub can be kept in the refrigerator for several months or in the bathroom for up to 1 week (make sure it's sealed tightly to avoid ants).

More and more companies are making brown sugar body scrubs, but why buy them when they are dead easy to make at home? I like to make it even more aromatic with a vanilla bean. The longer the vanilla bean and sugar are stored together, the stronger the vanilla fragrance will be.

After-Bath Oil

֍ Makes about 1 cup

1 cup of your favorite oil
(I like coconut, olive, or
argan oil)

10 to 12 drops lavender
essential oil

֍ Simply mix the oils in an airtight container and store in a cool, dry place.

This oil is great for adding deep body moisture after a bath or shower. I recommend applying this before you dry off so it seeps into all your pores.

Avocado Hair Mask

᥍ Makes 1 treatment

1 ripe avocado

2 tablespoons coconut oil, warmed so it's liquid

1 tablespoon honey

3 to 5 drops essential oil (I like gardenia)

᥍ Cut the avocado in half and scoop the pulp into a bowl. Mash the pulp with a fork, and stir in the coconut oil, honey, and essential oil. Apply generously to your hair, paying extra attention to the ends. Put on a shower cap and leave the mask on anywhere from 5 to 30 minutes. Wash out as you normally would with your favorite shampoo.

Dry hair—especially the ends—happens to everyone, but this mask can help. In my ideal world, I like to rub this mask into my hair, pile it all into a shower cap, and read a book for 30 minutes. These opportunities are all too rare, so it's a good thing that the mask can work most of its magic in 5 minutes, if that's all there's time for.

Coconut Oil Chest Rub

᥍ Makes about 1 ounce

2 tablespoons coconut oil

5 drops eucalyptus oil

3 drops peppermint oil

᥍ Simply combine the ingredients in a small airtight container and store in a cool, dry place.

Make this oil to soothe a kid's cold or cough (or your own). It makes a small amount, but a little goes a long way.

Kitchen Notebook

LET'S FACE IT: It's not always easy to find time to get to the grocery store. To make sure I stay a step ahead, I keep my pantry stocked with a variety of oils, condiments, cans of tomatoes, pasta, dried herbs and spices—the list goes on. So, when family or friends drop in at the last minute, I have enough on hand to put together a meal for everyone.

Although I've changed coasts and cities a few times in my life, I have always believed in the importance of a well-stocked pantry. Some ingredients have always been part of the mix (hot sauce, soy sauce), while others are new favorites I've adopted since living in the San Francisco Bay Area (hello, coconut oil!).

I've divided my pantry list into two sections: the need-to-have ingredients and the nice-to-have ones. The need-to-have ingredients are the ones that I use *all the time* (extra-virgin olive oil). These are the things I don't hesitate to load up on at the store when I'm running low. The nice-to-have ingredients are the ones that I keep around to help me avoid getting stuck in a cooking rut (capers, artichoke hearts, farro).

While they might not be the first things I reach for, I rely on them to
keep me excited about cooking. Together, these two categories set me
up for success.

Oils, Vinegars, Condiments

Need to have	*Extra-virgin olive oil*	I love the freshness of olive oil and its versatility (I even use it in my hair). Even though it's not an ideal high-heat cooking oil, sometimes I use it over high heat because I love the flavor. I have a few olive trees at my home, and I can't wait to find out what kind of olive oil they'll be able to yield.
	Canola oil	This actually *is* the ideal high-heat cooking oil. It's essential for frying.
	Hot sauce	I like Tapatío and Crystal, but my dad swears by Frank's RedHot. Pick whatever hot sauce you like best.
	Soy sauce/tamari	I prefer low-sodium soy sauce because if you can cut out a little salt, why not? Tamari is great when I need a gluten-free alternative for family or friends.
	Mirin	This sweet-tasting rice wine adds a nice touch to marinades and fish, especially salmon. Sometimes I'll throw it into a cooking or dipping sauce to add a little sweetness. Check the label to see if it requires refrigeration.
	Vinegars, especially distilled white vinegar, red wine vinegar, and balsamic vinegar	Vinegar is so useful in cooking—and cleaning. Put a little white vinegar in a spray bottle and fill it with water. Now you have an all-natural, all-purpose cleaner.

{ Nice to have }	*Bitters*	Although it's usually used to make cocktails, the complex medley of spices found in one bottle can add an edge to everything from Mango Lemonade (page 191) to Amaretto Pound Cake with Lemon Glaze (see page 204).
	Chili oil	This might actually fall into the "need to have" category for me. I use it extensively with fish and shrimp, and even with fruit salad when I want a little dash of heat. Look for chili oil in the Asian ingredients section of your grocery store. I use Lee Kum Kee brand.
	Sweet chili sauce	This spicy-sweet condiment is essential for my Sweet Chili Shrimp Wraps (page 78). Thai Kitchen makes one that's widely available.
	Fish sauce	Because sometimes you need to add a little funk.
	Oyster sauce	This is one of my dad's "secret" ingredients for his meatloaf (page 154), though not anymore.... Look for it in the Asian ingredients section of your grocery store near the fish sauce and the chili oil.
	Coconut oil	I cook with coconut oil, but I also use it in my hair—how can you resist the aroma?
	Grapeseed oil	I like to use this neutral-tasting oil in salad dressings when I'm not using olive oil. It can also be used for high-heat frying.
	Truffle oil	A splash of this every now and again hits the spot. A little goes a long way.
	Worcestershire	A bottle of Worcestershire will keep in your pantry forever. It's great for marinades.

Salt, Pepper, Herbs, Spices, etc.

Need to have	*Kosher salt*	I prefer Diamond Crystal; its granules are a little finer than other brands.
	Black pepper	I keep a pepper mill filled with black peppercorns so it can be ground fresh each time I use it.
	Dried chile flakes	
	Italian seasoning blend	This versatile mixture usually contains some combination of dried basil, marjoram, oregano, rosemary, sage, savory, and thyme.
	A selection of ground and whole spices	I always have ground allspice, cayenne, cinnamon, cloves, ginger, nutmeg, and paprika in my pantry. I keep ground cinnamon and cinnamon sticks on hand for both sweet and savory dishes. (See the Caribbean Seasonings section for more details.)
	Garlic, garlic powder, and garlic salt	What can I say? I like options.
	Onions and shallots	

Nice to have	*A selection of specialty salts*	I sprinkle flaky sea salt (such as Maldon) on top of steak or seared scallops for a salty crunch. Grated pink Himalayan salt has a subtle mineral flavor—and it looks pretty.
	Spike Vege-Sal Magic!	Who needs MSG when you can use Vege-Sal? Made up of ground vegetables mixed with salt, it's a super flavorful seasoning that you can use in place of plain salt. It's also good on avocado toast—really, really good on avocado toast.
	Pink peppercorns	I love using pink peppercorns in my Honey-Pepper Shrimp (page 122). (They are also surprisingly good in some desserts, but I leave that use to the pros.)
	White pepper	I use white pepper with lighter, creamy sauces and soups so the color of the dish looks polished. It's a pro tip I picked up at the San Francisco Cooking School. I buy white pepper pre-ground so I don't get confused with two separate pepper mills on the counter.

Caribbean Seasonings

Dried spices are not just for baking! The Caribbean food my mom cooks is packed with spices and chiles. Jamaican jerk seasoning goes heavy on Scotch bonnet peppers and many familiar "baking" spices. When my mom cooks island-style meals, these seasonings are usually within reach:

Need to have		
	Yellow curry powder	I like Grace or Betapac, which are brands of Jamaican curry. They're never very expensive, but a word of caution: they can be spicier than other curry powder brands. A good second option are the packets of Madras curry powder sold in Asian grocery stores.
	Hot peppers	Go for Scotch bonnets (those small but fiery orange peppers) if you can take the heat, jalapeños if you need something on the milder side.
	Fresh ginger	
	Garlic	
	Green onions	
	Fresh thyme	
	Ground and whole cloves	
	Ground allspice	
	Ground nutmeg	
	Black pepper	
	Soy sauce	
	Vinegar	

Cans and Jars

{ Need to have	*Canned whole San Marzano tomatoes*	I buy whole tomatoes whenever possible—they tend to be of better quality than tomatoes that are already chopped. To crush tomatoes, pour them into a bowl and squish them with your hands. It's a good job for the littles. (An apron might come in handy.)
	Canned beans	Black beans, kidney beans, pinto beans, chickpeas, you name it.
	Tomato paste	
	Tuna packed in oil	Oil-packed tuna is richer, with better flavor than water-packed tuna.
	Salsa	Pick your favorite. Salsa is definitely a "need to have" in my house.
	Broth	I use mostly chicken broth, but beef and vegetable broth also come in handy.
	Fruit preserves	I stock a variety of flavors, like apricot, peach, strawberry, and fig.

These are the ingredients that save the day when I need to throw together a pasta dish at the last minute:

{ Nice to have	*Sardines*	
	Capers	
	Olives	
	Canned artichoke hearts	
	Roasted red peppers	
	Sun-dried tomatoes	

Pasta, Grains, and Legumes

Need to have		
Dried beans of all kinds		
Pasta	I keep thin spaghetti, macaroni, and egg noodles (essential for Stephen's Five-Ingredient Pasta, page 158) on hand at all times.
Jasmine rice	
Sushi rice	I love the sticky consistency of sushi rice. My Mirin and Soy Steak with Sushi Rice (page 156) is a nice break from meat and potatoes.
Oats	I stock both quick-cooking and steel-cut oats.

Nice to have		
Other pasta shapes	We also like bucatini, rigatoni, linguini, and orzo.
Quinoa	
Farro	
Brown rice	I probably should eat this more than I do, but I digress…
Breadcrumbs	I especially like panko.

Baking

{ Need to have }	All-purpose flour	
	Dark brown sugar	In case you haven't noticed, I add this to just about everything.
	Honey	We harvest honey from our own hives! It's amazing stuff.
	Granulated sugar	I tend to use baker's superfine sugar, but regular granulated works, too.
	Natural cane sugar/ turbinado	I put this in my coffee.
	Active dry or instant yeast	
	Baking powder	
	Baking soda	It's a "need to have" not only in baking but also in your refrigerator to absorb odors and keep any weird smells under control.
	Cornstarch	
	Pure vanilla extract	Get the real stuff. No imitation, please!
	Nuts	Store a selection of nuts—almonds, walnuts, and pecans—in the freezer to keep them from turning rancid.
	Dried fruit	We rely mostly on raisins, dates, and dried cherries, apricots, and cranberries.

{ Nice to have }	Pure almond extract	I use a few drops in my pancake batter.
	Confectioners' sugar	
	Stevia drops	This goes into my Power Coffee (page 10) if I'm cutting out the turbinado sugar.
	Ground flaxseed	It's a good idea to store flaxseed in the freezer to keep it fresh.
	Chia seeds	I sneak these into my family's breakfast sometimes. Don't tell.
	Gluten-free flour	Both King Arthur and Cup4Cup make a gluten-free flour that you can sub in for regular all-purpose flour in most recipes.
	Whole-wheat flour	

In the Fridge

Need to have		
Whole milk	I'm not a fan of nonfat dairy, ever.
Heavy cream	
Butter	I use unsalted most of the time.
Large eggs	
Cheese	I keep Parmesan, Cheddar, and mozzarella on hand at all times.
Greek yogurt	Again, I go for whole milk here.
Nut butters	We use peanut and almond butter the most.
Orange juice	
Flour tortillas	I have yet to warm up to corn tortillas.
Mayonnaise/Vegenaise	I use these interchangeably. Vegenaise is the vegan version, but it's so delicious you don't feel like you're missing out.
Maple syrup	The real stuff needs to be refrigerated. Buying maple syrup is a big argument in my household. I buy *only* pure maple syrup, but Stephen likes Aunt Jemima.
Apples	
Bananas	Here's a cool thing to do: Cut up bananas that are a little too ripe, put them in sealable bags, and stick them in the freezer. If you want to make a healthy ice cream, you take the frozen bananas, add more fruit, blend it, and then freeze it in an ice cream maker.
Limes	
Lemons	
Oranges	
Carrots	
Spinach	This puts the "green" in my Island Green Smoothie (page 187).

Nice to have	Half-and-half	
	Almond milk (Or try making your own! See page 183.)	
	Other fresh fruit juices	
	Fresh pineapple	
	Bacon	
	Ketchup	
	Dijon mustard	

In the Freezer

Need to have	Frozen berries	I like to have a combination of raspberries, blackberries, blueberries, and strawberries.
	Frozen peas	
	Frozen spinach	
	Vanilla ice cream	This can save the day sometimes.
	Ground beef	We always keep this around to make Game Day Pasta (page 100).
	Whole chicken breasts	

Nice to have	Frozen tropical fruit for smoothies	Think mangos and pineapples.
	Ground turkey	
	Whole turkey breasts	
	Pancetta	

WHAT'S IN MY KITCHEN?

My go-to pots and pans

Le Creuset cookware
Vitamix blender
Williams-Sonoma Goldtouch
   bakeware
KitchenAid mixer
Great set of knives
Cutting board
Mixing bowls
Wooden mixing spoons
Fish spatula
Zester
Cocktail shaker (because yes!)

Acknowledgments

MY HUSBAND, STEPHEN: Thank you for being my guinea pig and ultimate supporter. You have been the driving force behind everything I do, and you always push me and motivate me to conquer things more than my little mind could have dreamed.

Mom and Dad: Thank you for instilling the gift of love in me from a young age and never letting me settle or think I couldn't be whoever I wanted to be. Mom, my tireless work ethic comes from you, and I thank you for that. Dad, my passion, joy, and fearlessness come from you, and I am forever grateful.

My girls: Thank you for being cute and carefree and happy. You inspire me every second of the day. It's so much fun getting to be a kid again through your eyes.

Carolyn: Thank you for taking the best care of my little girls while I'm working. This year has been an adjustment for me with my career and transitioning to having two little ones. You are such a blessing, and I feel overjoyed knowing that I don't have to worry and that my girls are cared for. It truly does take a village.

My grandma Gwendolyn: Thank you for blessing our family with the gift of our Jamaican culture. I feel so lucky to have a little island flavor in my blood.

My in-laws, Sonya and Dell (aka Grashi and G-daddy): Thank you for raising the sweetest, most kind and humble man on the planet.

Caroline Egan: Thank you for your vision and support through this whole process. Years ago we sat at our favorite neighborhood eatery and spoke of our hopes and dreams. They've all come true, and I am so happy to have worked with you on this book and to have you as a friend. The images are gorgeous and reflect all our hard work. You've tried my food and now "you know who I am." (Ha!)

My team at Flutie Management: Thank you all for your hard work and support. You guys have helped in making all my dreams come true. I couldn't have done it without you.

Stacey Glick: Thank you so much for being the best literary agent on the face of the planet and helping me find my publishing home.

Amanda Haas and the girls at Williams-Sonoma: Thank you for making me feel like a rock star and treating me so well. You always go above and beyond for me!

My Little, Brown and Company family: Thank you for believing in my vision and having as much passion for the book as I could have hoped for. You guys are simply amazing and a dream to work with. I also want to thank you all for the creative freedom.

John Parsley at Little, Brown: Thank you for being the coolest VP/Editor everrrrr.

My recipe testers, Melissa Stewart and Sandra Wu, and my book manager Kate Leahy: Thank you for getting it right and making me look semi-professional. I couldn't have done it without you all.

All the strong, beautiful, and God-fearing women who have inspired me all throughout my life: Thank you!

Index

About the Author

AYESHA CURRY has been featured in *Food & Wine*, *Time*, *InStyle*, *Cooking Light*, the *Wall Street Journal*, *People*, and *USA Today* and is a frequent guest on *The Rachael Ray Show*. Curry has appeared on several popular Food Network programs and hosts her own show on the Cooking Channel. Mom to two daughters, Riley and Ryan, and wife to Stephen Curry, she lives in the Bay Area.